First published in 1989 by

Young Library Ltd
The Old Brushworks
56 Pickwick Road
Corsham, Wiltshire SN13 9BX

© Copyright 1989 Young Library Ltd
Text: © Copyright 1989 Suzi Clarke
Patterns: © Copyright 1989 Carole Hersee
Illustrations: © Copyright 1989 Carol Wainwright
All rights reserved

ISBN 0 946003 86 6

Printed and bound in Hong Kong

CONTENTS

Introduction *5–8*
   Fabrics *6*
   Patterns *6*
   Measuring *6*

Fitting Guide *9*
   Making the pattern *9*
      Bodices and jackets 10
      Sleeves 10
      Petticoats 10
      Waists 10
      Coats 10
      Fabric amounts 11

Evening Bodice *12*

Closed Bodice *14*

Berthas *15*
   1835 bertha *15*
   1842 bertha *15*
   1865 bertha *15*

Sleeves *16*
   Evening puff sleeve 1835 *16*
   Gathered sleeve 1835–40 *16*
   Pagoda sleeve *16*
      Sleeve puff for pagoda sleeve 16
   Evening sleeve 1842–65 *18*
   Plain sleeve 1840–65 *18*
   Cuffs *18–19*

Girl's jacket *21–2*

Boy's cropped jacket *24*

Man's coat or Uniform jacket *26*

Skirts for Men's coats and jackets *27*
   Coat skirt *27*
   Uniform jacket skirt *27*
   Coat tails *28*

Collars *30–31*
   Large collar *30*
   Stand collar *31*
   Peter Pan collar *31*
   Pelerine collar *31*

Trousers *33*

Crinoline *34–6*
   Crinoline pad *35*
   Crinoline frills *36*

Petticoat *39*

Skirts *39*
   Plain skirt *39*
   Skirt with two frills *39*
   Double skirt *40*
   Shaped skirt with three frills *40*

Pantaloons *43*

Glossary *44*

Index *48*

4 **Evening dress, 1835**

Woman's buttercup evening dress, about 1835
Evening bodice with evening puff sleeves and bertha. Plain skirt over petticoat.

INTRODUCTION

Clothes changed a great deal during the reign of Queen Victoria who was on the throne for sixty-four years from 1837 to 1901. In this book we look at the clothes worn during the earlier half of her reign, from about 1837 to about 1865.

During the first thirty or forty years of the nineteenth century, fashions changed quite slowly. Styles changed more rapidly later, particularly among the fashionable women who lived in the big towns and cities. Men's clothes became plainer, although wealthy men wore suits made of very expensive material. Fashionable men and women had a different set of clothes for every occasion.

There were several reasons for the rapid changes of style. Machinery began to be used for work previously done by hand. Yarn could be spun far more quickly by machine than it could by hand. Weaving machines wove the yarn into cloth. It was far easier and quicker to make clothes after the invention of the lockstitch sewing machine in 1846.

The growth of other industries also affected fashions. Magazines were published showing pictures of the latest styles. The new railway network, and faster and more comfortable ships, meant that people travelled more. Ideas about fashion, and copies of fashion magazines, were taken to other countries such as America and Australia. Dressmakers and tailors were able to copy the clothes worn by fashionable travellers. Clothes and cloth were also exported.

The first fashion pictures were drawings. These were later supplemented by photographs. Photographs give us a good idea of what people actually wore at the time, rather than the styles fashion magazines thought they should wear.

Ladies wore full skirts, supported in various ways. Between 1835 and 1856 skirts were held out by full petticoats. The petticoats had frills to make them even fuller. After 1856 skirts were often supported by a crinoline, which was a kind of cage-shaped petticoat stiffened with steel wire. The dresses in this book can be held out either by a crinoline or by lots of petticoats.

Bodices were usually fitted, but the shape of the sleeves changed a great deal during this period. In the early years the sleeves were very large and full. They gradually became smaller and tight-fitting, and then fuller again but in a different style from the early full sleeves.

Girls wore similar clothes to women, but they also began to have fashions of their own. Small girls usually wore skirts to just below the knee, often showing the lace edge of a petticoat. Underneath they wore 'drawers', 'pantaloons', or 'pantalettes', which were long-legged knickers with lace edges. The legs of the drawers showed below the petticoat. Older girls wore skirts to just above the ankle, often with the lace edges of the drawers showing. Girls were used to wearing corsets from a very early age.

Small boys wore dresses until they were about five or six years old. They also wore drawers underneath, but the dresses were usually plainer than those worn by girls. Older boys and young men wore straight trousers which finished above the ankle, and a short jacket or a longer, skirted tunic which was often worn belted. Older men's clothes were padded and stiffened, but these tailored clothes are not included in this book for they are complicated to make. It is usually possible to hire or borrow suitable costumes. A pattern for a uniform jacket is included, but it is not as stiff or as complicated as a real uniform jacket would be. All these clothes are illustrated in this book.

Hairstyles for both men and women changed with the fashions, as the illustrations show. Women usually had long hair worn in a variety of styles, ranging from the very elaborate and high style of 1835 to the smooth and simple styles of the 1840s and 1850s. Men wore their hair fairly long, often with 'sideboards' or long hair in front of the ears. Moustaches in various styles were fashionable. It is important to match hairstyles, hats, and other accessories to the costumes. Pictures of the period should be studied carefully to make sure all the details are correct.

Fabrics

The early Victorians used many different fabrics, in a range of colours and patterns. It should not be too difficult to reproduce these for your clothes. Plaids or tartans, floral materials, and stripes, were all very popular. Dresses could be trimmed in many ways. The best way to decide on the right trimming is to look at pictures in books, paintings, and old photographs. You can also see real clothes in museums and art galleries. However, people do not always agree about costumes' proper names. Those in this book might be called by different names elsewhere.

The ten colour illustrations each show a complete outfit. You can produce any number of further outfits simply by choosing different patterns for bodices, sleeves, skirts, etc. which are given in separate sections of the book. You may make your own selection of garments and put them together for the effect you want. Plan the whole outfit carefully before you begin.

Patterns

A dress pattern is a plan drawing of the garment to be made. It is drawn to the same size as the garment, then pinned to the fabric and used as a guide in cutting the required shapes.

All the patterns in this book are drawn on to a grid pattern of blue squares. Each side of a square represents two centimetres. Therefore, if the pattern shows a line extending for seven squares, it means it should be fourteen centimetres in length.

All measurements throughout are in centimetres, marked 'cm'.

This is the key to the various line markings on the patterns:

— — — — — — —
fold of fabric

— — — — — —
lengthening or shortening line

—·—·—·—·—·—
alternative cutting line

⊓⊓⊓⊓⊓⊓⊓
bone line

o o o o o o o
button positions

Most patterns are shown in two sizes — Size A in black, and Size B in red, according to the measurements below:

	GIRLS		BOYS	
	SIZE A	SIZE B	SIZE A	SIZE B
CHEST	72.5	81	71	81
WAIST	62	65	64	69
HIPS	76	87	75	84
NECK TO WAIST	33	37	32.5	38
HEIGHT	142	155	137	157

Obviously children in any age-group come in various shapes and sizes, so these measurements are a rough guide only.

Measuring

Take measurements with the person standing straight, and wearing thin garments such as a T-shirt and tights or briefs. However, if making a coat, measure over a thick jumper. Wear the shoes to be worn with the costume to get the 'length to ground' correct.

CHEST   Measure under arms round fullest part of chest.

WAIST   Tie a piece of string or tape round middle and bend person sideways to make string settle at proper waist; then measure over the string.

Day dress, 1837   7

Young woman's tan day dress, about 1837
Closed bodice with gathered sleeves and pelerine collar. Plain skirt over petticoat and pantaloons.

8 Introduction

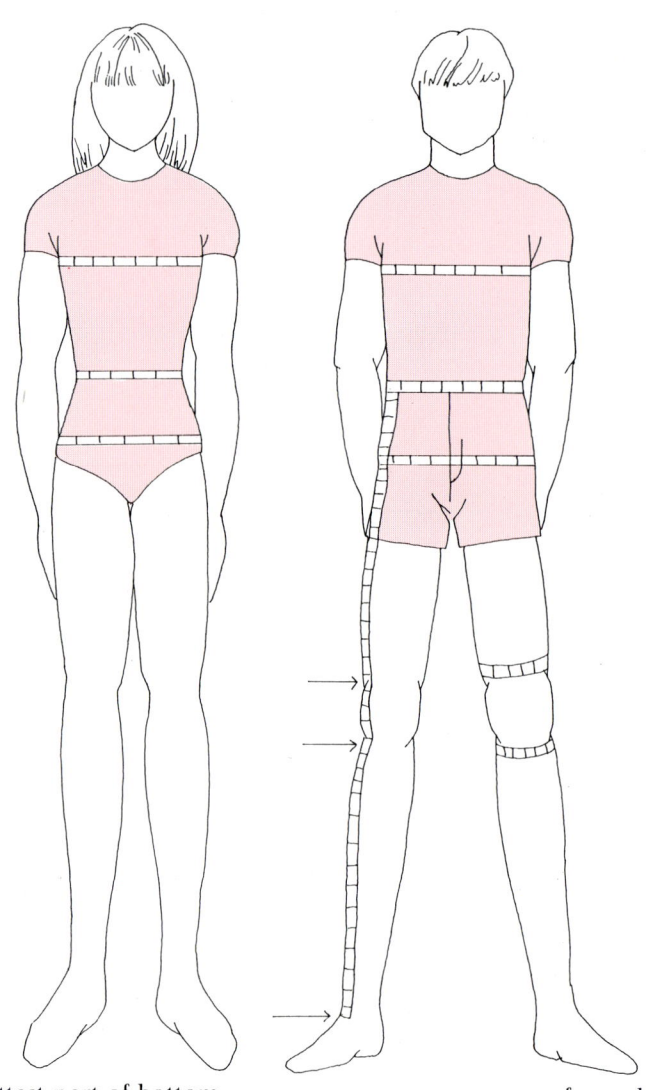

HIPS   Measure over fattest part of bottom.
THIGH   Measure where shown on diagram.
KNEE   Measure above or below knee as shown on diagram.
NECK   Measure round base of neck.

Add 2cm to each of the above measurements to allow for ease of fit.

LEG LENGTH   Measure from waist, over hip and down the leg to the required length, as shown on diagram. If measuring to below the knee, add 10cm to allow for sitting down.

NECK TO WAIST   Measure down the back from the base of neck to string marking waist.

NECK TO GROUND   Measure down the back from base of neck to ground.

SHOULDER   Measure across the back from base of neck to bone at outer shoulder.

ARM LENGTH   With bent arm, measure from bone at outer shoulder to elbow, then to wrist, as shown in diagram.

ARM GIRTH   Measure round upper arm, forearm, and wrist with finger inside tape to allow for ease of fit.

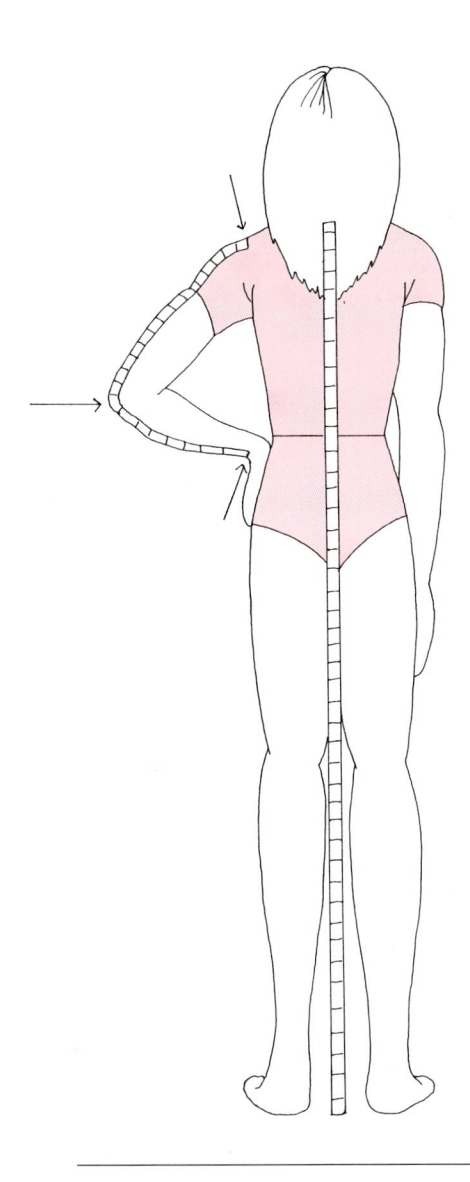

FITTING GUIDE

Making the pattern

To get a really good fit, and to avoid any mistakes when cutting out the fabric, it is essential to first draw out the pattern to full size, on squared paper which is obtainable from dressmaking shops. Then make up the garment first using calico, old sheeting, or other cheap material. You then alter the cheap calico pattern to fit the wearer. Finally you use the calico garment as the pattern on which to cut out the expensive fabric from which the garment is to be made. Think of it in eight stages:

1. Draw pattern to full size on squared paper, adding turnings of 2cm (or as indicated on the specific pattern) on all seams, and 7.5cm on hem. Cut out paper pattern.
2. Pin the paper pattern to calico, and cut out.
3. Using tracing wheel and dressmakers' tracing paper, trace all pattern outlines and markings on to wrong side of calico.

4　Make up according to the specific pattern instructions.

5　Fit the calico garment to the wearer, and mark any necessary alterations. Make sure you fit all parts of the costume in calico *at the same time*; that the armholes and neck are the right size; and that the length of sleeves and hem is correct.

6　When you are quite sure that all the necessary alterations have been marked clearly on the calico, remove it from the wearer and take it apart.

7　Make the alterations carefully, and if you are still not certain of the fit, check it on the wearer again.

8　Now you can use the calico as a pattern for the final version of the garment.

It all sounds rather complicated written down like this. But take it one stage at a time and it should be quite easy. Beginners always want to start making the final costume right away, but a little trouble at this stage might avoid a disaster later!

BODICES AND JACKETS

When fitting a calico bodice, make sure that it fits quite tightly, with no wrinkles if possible. The bodices in the patterns are boned because corsets are extremely difficult to make, and modern girls and women find them uncomfortable. If the bodice is fitted inside out it is easier to alter the seams. Boys' and young men's jackets should fit well but not tightly. Check the following points and mark any alterations on the calico in soft pencil or dressmakers' chalk.

1　Make sure that the bodice or jacket fits all round. To make it tighter or looser, alter the straight underarm seam.

2　Check the length of the bodice. It should fit just in to the natural waist at the sides. If the waist is pointed, it should not be too long. The waist of skirted jackets should fit comfortably in to the natural waist.

3　Check that the armholes fit properly and are neither too tight nor too loose. If the bodice has a low neck, check that it does not gape, and adjust the shoulder seam if necessary. If the garment has a high neck or a collar, make sure it is in the right place and is not uncomfortably high or low. Also make sure that the neckline is not too tight or too loose.

SLEEVES

It should be sufficient to make only one of each type of sleeve for a fitting. Check for length and tightness. Make sure it fits properly into the armhole, and hangs correctly for the sleeve you are making.

PETTICOATS

If using a crinoline, make sure that the petticoat is full enough to fit over it and that the skirt is full enough to fit over both of them. Also check that the hem of the dress is longer than the petticoat, and that the hem of the crinoline does not show under the petticoat. This also applies if using a petticoat stiffened with frills.

WAISTS

Check that the waists of the petticoat and crinoline fit firmly, otherwise the weight of the fabric may cause them to drop slightly. Should this happen, the petticoat and crinoline can each be held up with elastic braces. These are easily made from a length of 2.5cm elastic for each brace. Cut a buttonhole 5cm from each end and attach suitable buttons to the waistband.

COATS

If making a coat to fit over a costume, wear the costume while fitting the coat, or you may find that it is too small when made up.

FABRIC AMOUNTS

Bodice: 0.75m at 90cm width.
Jacket: 0.75m at 90cm width plus extra for skirts as required.
Plain sleeves: 0.75m at 90cm width; for other sleeves see pattern.
Skirt/petticoat: 3m at 90cm width, 115cm, or 122cm, depending on the fullness of the skirt, but check the length carefully.
Trousers/pantaloons: 1m at 90cm width.

Day dress, about 1858   11

Lady's lilac three-tier day dress, about 1858
Closed bodice with pagoda sleeves and pagoda sleeve puffs. Skirt with three frills over crinoline and petticoat.

EVENING BODICE

A bodice is the top part of a lady's dress. The basic evening dress bodice is illustrated in the picture of the buttercup evening dress of 1835 (page 4).

It can be used for costumes throughout the Early Victorian period. You merely need to adjust the waistline as necessary, and use an appropriate trimming. For example, the ladies' dresses of 1842 and 1858 (pages 38 and 11) which have pointed waist lines, are both adaptations of this basic bodice pattern.

The bodice should have a boned lining to give the appearance of being worn over a corset. Evening dresses were usually made of fabrics such as silk, satin, taffeta, or lace, but it is possible to buy inexpensive substitutes for these fabrics. Some cottons are also suitable. The lining should be of cotton drill, sheeting (not poly-cotton), or bleached calico.

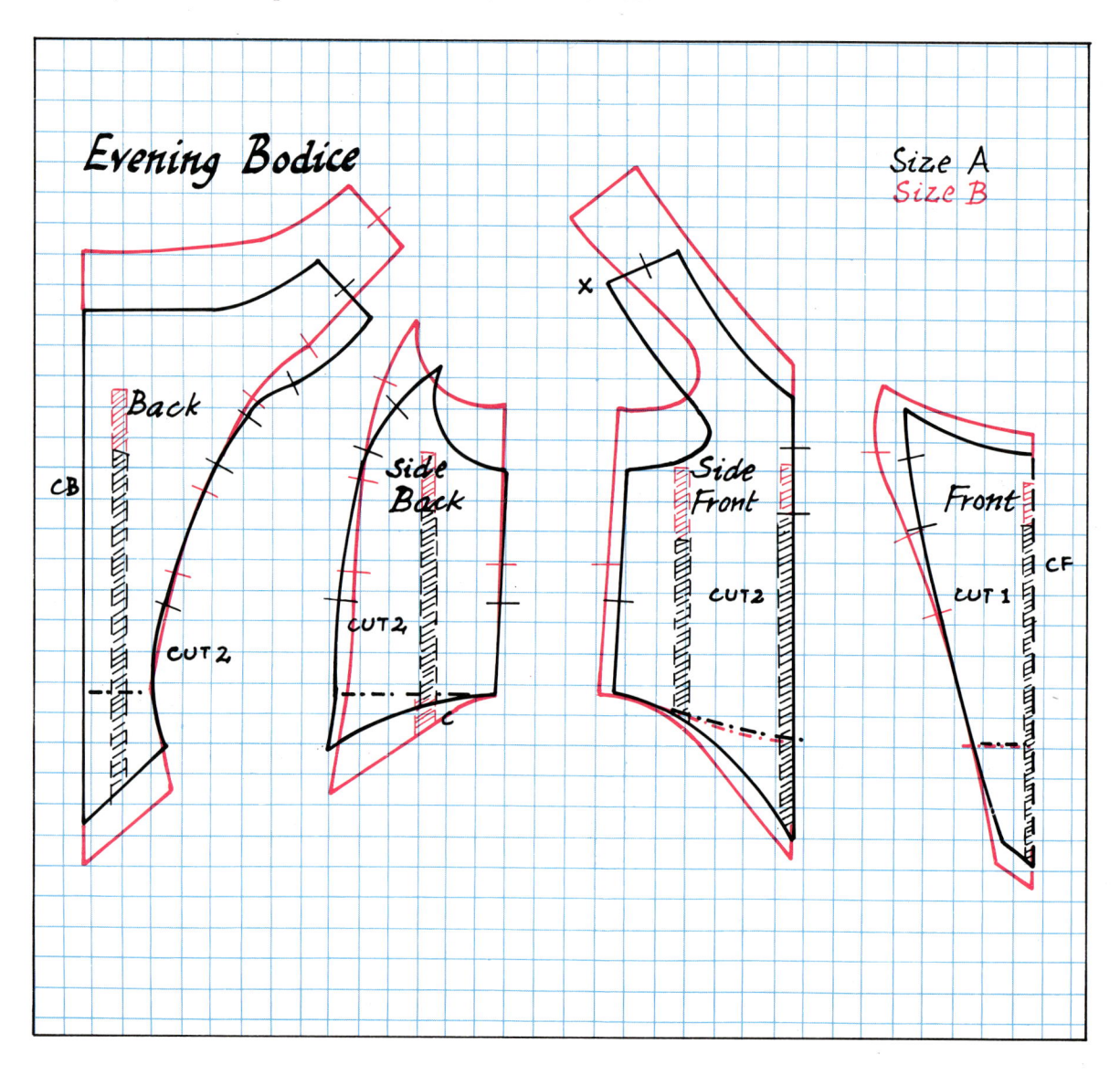

Evening bodice

1. Make calico pattern as instructed in Fitting Guide, adding turnings of 2cm at neck, armhole edges and waist seams, and 5cm to back and side seams.
2. Using the altered calico as a pattern, cut out the lining fabric.
3. Use a tracing wheel and dressmakers' tracing paper to trace pattern outlines and markings on to right side of lining fabric, and trace the bone lines on to the wrong side of the lining fabric.
4. Use this as a pattern. Pin to main fabric and cut out. Make sure the pieces are the right way round, and that you have right and left sides, right and left sleeves etc.
5. Sew Rigilene along bone lines on wrong side of lining material, stopping 1cm short of the waist line.
6. Wrong sides together, tack main fabric to lining material just outside seam lines, and use as one fabric.
7. Right sides together and matching balance marks, join side fronts to front.
8. Right sides together and matching balance marks, join side backs to backs. The seam should be curved.
9. Right sides together and matching balance marks, join side fronts to side backs.
10. Right sides together and matching balance marks, join shoulder seams.
11. Clip curves and zig-zag or oversew raw edges to neaten.
12. Press all seams open.
13. Check the fitting again, over the skirt and petticoat or crinoline to which it belongs. Make sure that the bodice waist is big enough to fit over the thickness of the skirt waist. Alter the bodice if necessary.
14. Bias bind neck edge and waist edge of bodice.
15. Neaten back edges with zig-zag stitch or oversewing.
16. Put a row of stitches down both centre backs 5cm from edges.
17. Turn in right back edge 5cm and edge stitch, then catch down loose edge.
18. Sew on hooks 3–5cm apart.
19. Sew bars down left back line of stitches to match hooks.
20. Sew in sleeves (see pages 16–18 for sleeve instructions).
21. Attach bertha (see page 15 for bertha instructions).
22. Attach bodice to skirt (see page 39–40 for skirt instructions).

CLOSED BODICE

Like the Evening Bodice on page 12 this pattern can be used for several different styles of dress by varying the cut of the neck and waist. The girl's tan day dress of 1837 (page 7) needs a plain round neck and waist. The girl's pink-checked day dress of 1850 needs a square neck and pointed waist. The lilac dress of 1858 requires a round neck with pointed waist. Medium-weight fabrics are most suitable for this kind of dress.

1. Make calico pattern as instructed in Fitting Guide. Then use this pattern to cut out lining and main fabric, as for Evening Bodice (stages 2–4).
2. Bone lining fabric and tack to main fabric as for Evening Bodice (stages 5 and 6).
3. Stitch darts in both fronts.
4. Right sides together and matching balance marks, join sides to backs. The seam will be curved.

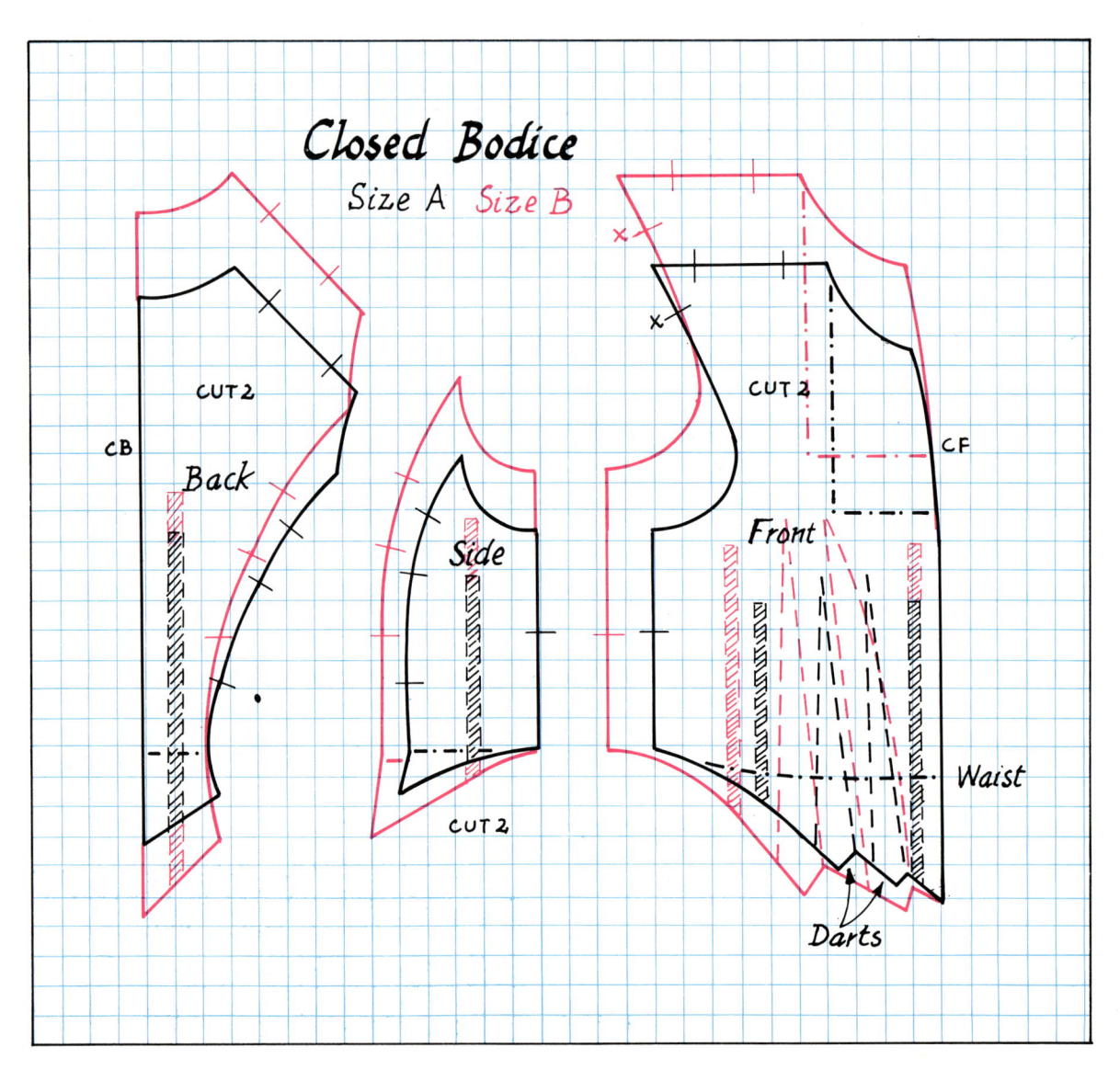

Closed Bodice
Size A   Size B

Back — CUT 2 — CB
Side — CUT 2
Front — CUT 2 — CF — Waist — Darts

5   Right sides together and matching balance marks, join centre front seam.
6   Right sides together and matching balance marks, join sides to fronts.
7   Right sides together and matching balance marks, join shoulder seams.
8   Complete bodice as for Evening Bodice (stages 11–22).

BERTHAS

A bertha (sometimes spelled berthe) was a soft collar which was usually worn over the top of an evening dress bodice. Berthas were often transparent, so could be made of lace, or the fabric of the dress if this was fine enough. They are very simple to make, and therefore do not need patterns.

1835 Bertha

This bertha can be seen in the picture of the buttercup evening dress on page 4. It should be cut on the crossway grain of the fabric.

1   Measure round neckline from shoulder to centre front to other shoulder, and add 5cm.
2   Measure shoulder strap width and multiply by 3.
3   Add 2cm for turnings, and cut crossway fabric to these measurements.
4   Neaten raw edges, turn in 2cm all round, and hem.
5   Pleat ends to fit shoulder seam, and stitch down.
6   Stitch top centre front of bertha to top centre front of bodice.
7   Stretch pleats at centre front of bertha down centre front of bodice, and stitch down.
8   For back, measure from shoulder to centre back and add 2cm.
9   Repeat stages 2–5 for each side of back.
10 Stretch pleats down centre back edges a little, and stitch down, hiding fastenings if possible.
11 Stitch bows on shoulders to hide joins.

1842 Bertha

This bertha is simply a length of lace or transparent fabric. The picture of the green evening dress on page 38 shows a layer of lace over a slightly longer layer of fabric. Make up as one layer, as described.

1   Hold arms loosely at sides and measure over arms and body together. Multiply this figure by 2.
2   Decide depth of bertha and add 4cm for turnings. If the lace has a pretty border use this for the lower edge, and leave only 2cm for turnings.
3   Cut out, and neaten raw edges as necessary.
4   Repeat for second layer.
5   Pull gathers to fit neckline all round.
6   Fold gathers to inside of bodice neckline and stitch down. Cover with bias binding if required.

1865 Bertha

This is shown in the picture of the white evening dress on page 37. Cut a length of lace or transparent fabric to about twice the neckline measurement. Gather to fit the neckline, and trim in an appropriate style.

SLEEVES

The sleeve patterns given here can be fitted to various bodices to give the style you require. Check that the shape for the sleeve is correct for the dress by studying paintings or photos of the period. The sleeves should all be made of the same material as the dress, except for the sleeve puff for pagoda sleeve which should be made in a fine, semi-transparent material or broderie anglais.

Evening puff sleeve, 1835

An evening puff sleeve is shown on the buttercup evening dress on page 4.

1. Make calico pattern as instructed in Fitting Guide, adding 2cm turnings all round. Then use this pattern to cut out the fabric.
2. Use a tracing wheel and dressmakers' tracing paper to trace pattern outlines and markings on to wrong side of fabric.
3. Make two rows of gathering stitches between marks along top edge of sleeve.
4. Join sleeve seams, press open and neaten raw edges.
5. On wrong side of sleeve, stitch a length of India tape along guide line for elastic. Leave an opening to thread elastic.
6. Thread elastic, pull up to fit, overlap ends, and stitch firmly together. Stitch up opening.
7. Turn up hem, and stitch.
8. Pull up gathering threads on sleeve head to fit armhole and fasten off very securely.
9. Stitch sleeve in to armhole, matching 'x' on sleeve to 'x' on bodice, or to shoulder seam if there is no 'x' marked on pattern.
10. Neaten raw edges.

Gathered sleeve, 1835–40

A gathered sleeve is shown on the 1837 tan day dress illustrated on page 7. It is cut and made up in a similar way to the evening puff sleeve above.

1. Follow stages 1–4 of the evening puff sleeve pattern.
2. Several rows of gathering stitches should be put into the top of the sleeve between the marks. Four rows are marked on the pattern, but more may be used if required.
3. Finish by following stages 8–10 of evening puff sleeve. The wrist edge may be gathered into a cuff. Use the one-piece sleeve cuff pattern on page 20.
4. Join ends of cuff together to make a circle.
5. Right sides together, sew cuff to bottom edge of sleeve, turn to inside along fold line, and stitch down.

Pagoda sleeve, 1845–1865

A pagoda sleeve has a very wide opening. Examples can be seen on the day dresses shown on pages 11 and 41.

1. Make calico pattern as instructed in Fitting Guide, adding 2cm for turnings at top and sides, and 4cm for hem. Then use this pattern to cut out fabric.
2. Use a tracing wheel and dressmakers' tracing paper to trace pattern outlines and markings on to wrong side of fabric.
3. Right sides together and matching balance marks, join sleeve seams.
4. Press seams open and neaten raw edges.
5. Turn and stitch hem.
6. Stitch into armhole, matching 'x' on sleeve to 'x' on bodice, or to shoulder seam if there is no 'x' marked on your pattern.

SLEEVE PUFF FOR PAGODA SLEEVE

Sleeve puffs are shown on the pink-checked day dress on page 41. They were worn under any wide-wristed sleeves such as pagoda sleeves, to cover the arms during the day. They were not attached to the sleeve, but were held in place above the elbow by elastic.

Sleeves 17

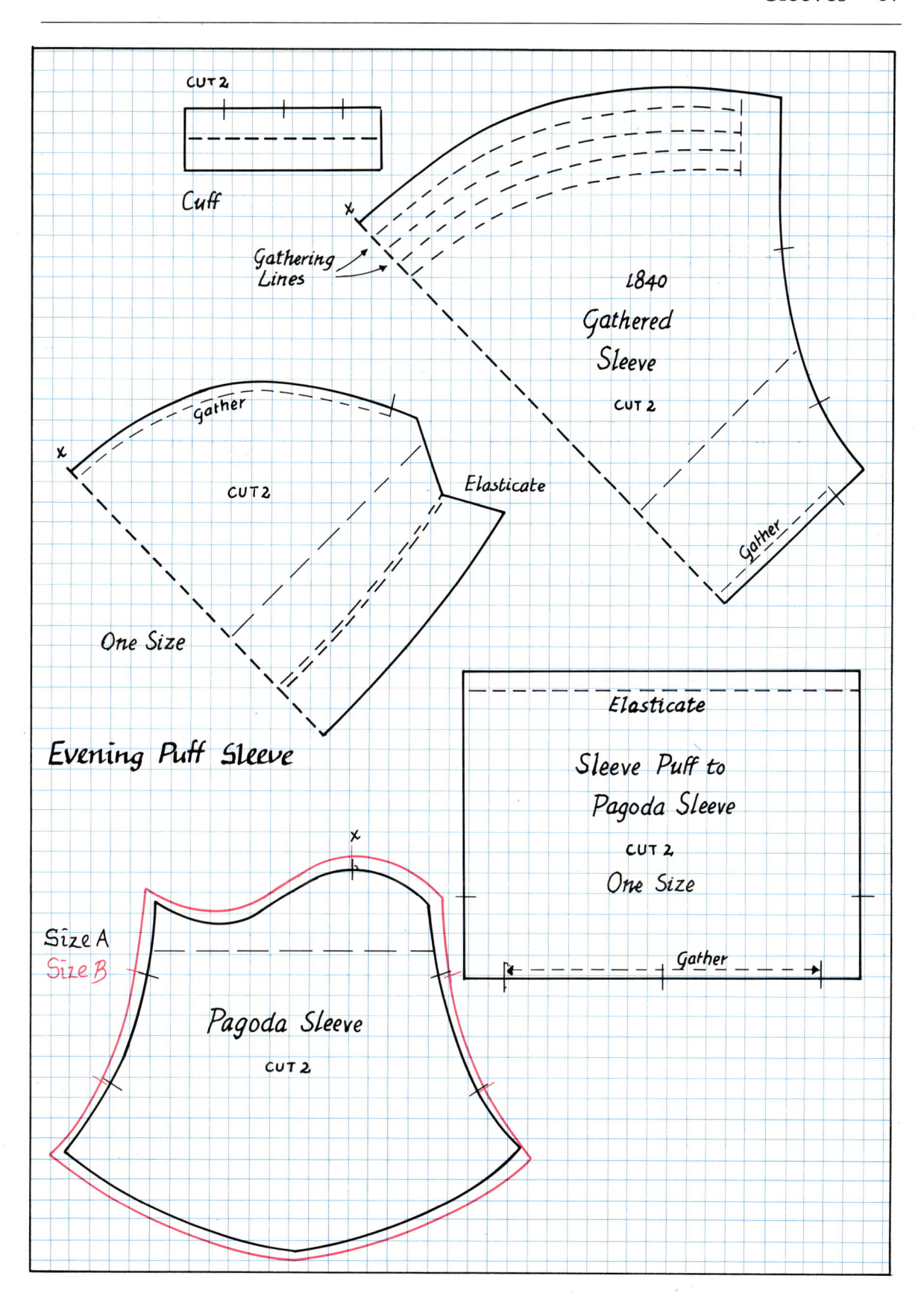

Sleeves

The puffs should be made in a lightweight, semi-transparent fabric. It should not be necessary to make a calico pattern first.

1. Make paper pattern, as instructed in Fitting Guide, adding 2cm turnings all round.
2. Use paper pattern to cut out main fabric.
3. Use a tracing wheel and dressmakers' tracing paper to trace pattern outlines and markings on to wrong side of fabric.
4. Right sides together and matching balance marks, join sleeve seams.
5. Press seams open and neaten raw edges.
6. Pull up gathering stitches to fit cuff.
7. Join ends of cuff together to make a circle.
8. Right sides together, sew cuff to bottom edge of sleeve, turn to inside along fold line and stitch down.
9. Turn a hem at top edge of sleeve to make a casing for elastic. Leave a gap for threading elastic.
10. Thread elastic through casing, pull up to fit, overlap ends and stitch firmly together.
11. Stitch up opening.

Evening sleeves 1842–1865

The green dress on page 38 shows an 'unshaped' evening sleeve. For the shaped version on the white dress on page 37, follow the V-shaped cutting line. Make up either version in exactly the same way as the pagoda sleeve. For the shaped version make a very narrow hem and turn up using bias binding.

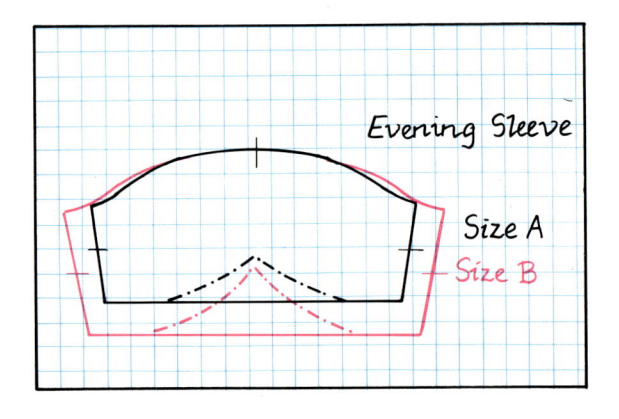

Plain sleeves, 1840–1865

Plain sleeves can be seen on the young woman's turquoise suit of 1845. They can be made in one-piece or two-piece versions.

The one-piece sleeve is also suitable for boys' jackets or coats, or the man's uniform jacket. If the uniform is to be made of felt and lined, the sleeves should be lined in the same way, but using a silky type of lining material. Cuffs may be added as shown below.

The two-piece sleeve is shaped more closely to the arm. It would be worn on a simple day dress with a pointed waist, or on a jacket. It is also suitable for some boys' coats or jackets.

ONE-PIECE VERSION

Make the one-piece version in exactly the same way as the pagoda sleeve.

TWO-PIECE VERSION

1. Make calico pattern as illustrated in Fitting Guide, adding 2cm for turnings all round. Then use this pattern to cut out the fabric.
2. Use a tracing wheel and dressmakers' tracing paper to trace pattern outlines and markings on to wrong side of fabric.
3. Right sides together and matching balance marks, join sleeve seams, press open, clip into curves and neaten raw edges.
4. Turn up wrist edge with bias binding.
5. Stitch into armhole, matching 'x' on sleeve to 'x' on bodice or jacket, or to shoulder seam if no 'x' is marked on the bodice or jacket pattern.

Cuffs

To make cuffs for the two-piece sleeve:

1. Make calico pattern as instructed in Fitting Guide.
2. Using corrected calico pattern, cut two cuffs for each sleeve. Cut both cuffs in main fabric, or cut one of fabric and one of lining fabric.
3. Stiffen with iron-on stiffening fabric such as 'Vilene' or canvas.

Evening Sleeve
Size A
Size B

Suit, about 1845 19

Girl's turquoise suit, about 1845
Jacket with collar, and two-piece sleeves with cuff. Plain skirt over crinoline or petticoat.

20 Sleeves

Plain Sleeves (two piece and one piece)

- 2 piece Sleeve — CUT 2
- 2 piece Sleeve — CUT 2
- 1 piece Sleeve — CUT 2
- Size A
- Size B

Cuffs

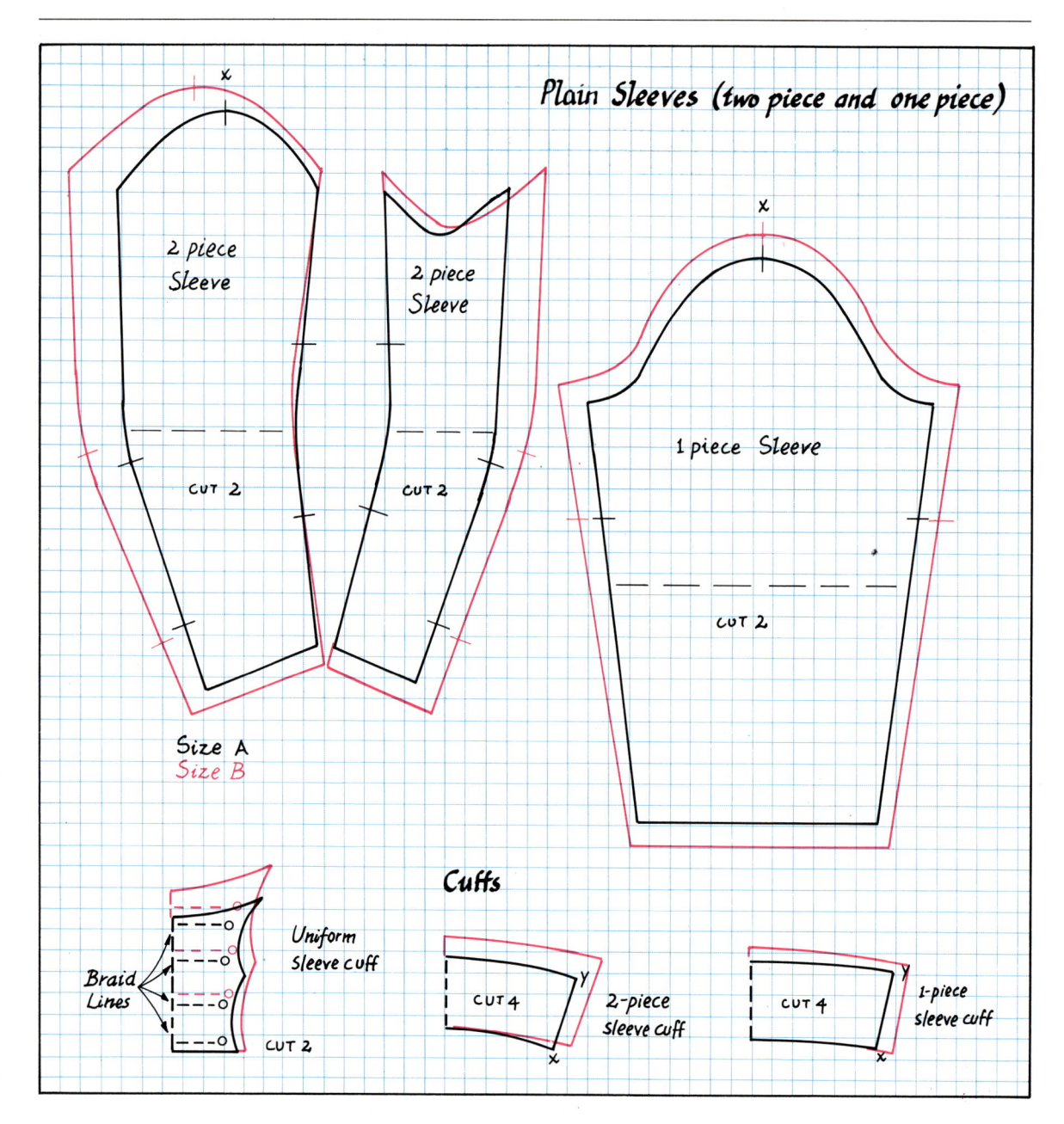

- Uniform Sleeve cuff — Braid Lines — CUT 2
- 2-piece sleeve cuff — CUT 4
- 1-piece sleeve cuff — CUT 4

4   Stitch cuffs, or cuff and lining, together from 'x' to 'y' across curve, and from 'y' to 'x'.
5   Clip corners, bag out, and press.
6   Turn hem to inside of cuff and stitch neatly.
7   Stitch cuff to sleeve end.

To make cuffs for the one-piece sleeve:

1   Follow stages 1–3 for cuff of the two-piece sleeve.
2   Stitch cuffs together from 'y' to 'y'.
3   Stitch seams from 'x' across 'y' to 'x'.
4   Turn cuff to right side and press.
5   Turn hem to inside and stitch neatly.
6   Stitch to sleeve end.

If the one-piece sleeve cuffs are intended for the uniform jacket:

1   Cut out shapes in felt or wool.
2   Wrong side of cuff to right side of sleeve, topstitch to sleeve (or if the uniform is made of felt, it may be possible to glue them on).
3   Stitch on gold or silver braid to conceal edges.

GIRL'S JACKET

A simple jacket of the kind seen in the turquoise suit on page 19 was worn from 1845 to 1865. In the early part of the period it would have had tight-fitting plain sleeves. In the latter part of the period it would have had pagoda sleeves.

Plain or patterned fabrics were used. They could be as thick as velvet or as fine as lace. The jacket and skirt should be made of the same material, and so should the facing on the front. The jacket should be lined, and the lining boned to look as if it is worn over a corset.

1. Make calico pattern as instructed in Fitting Guide, adding 2cm for turnings all round.
2. Follow stages 2–4 of the instructions for the Evening Bodice given on page 13.
3. To cut pattern for front facings, use corrected calico pattern for front. Draw a line 5cm

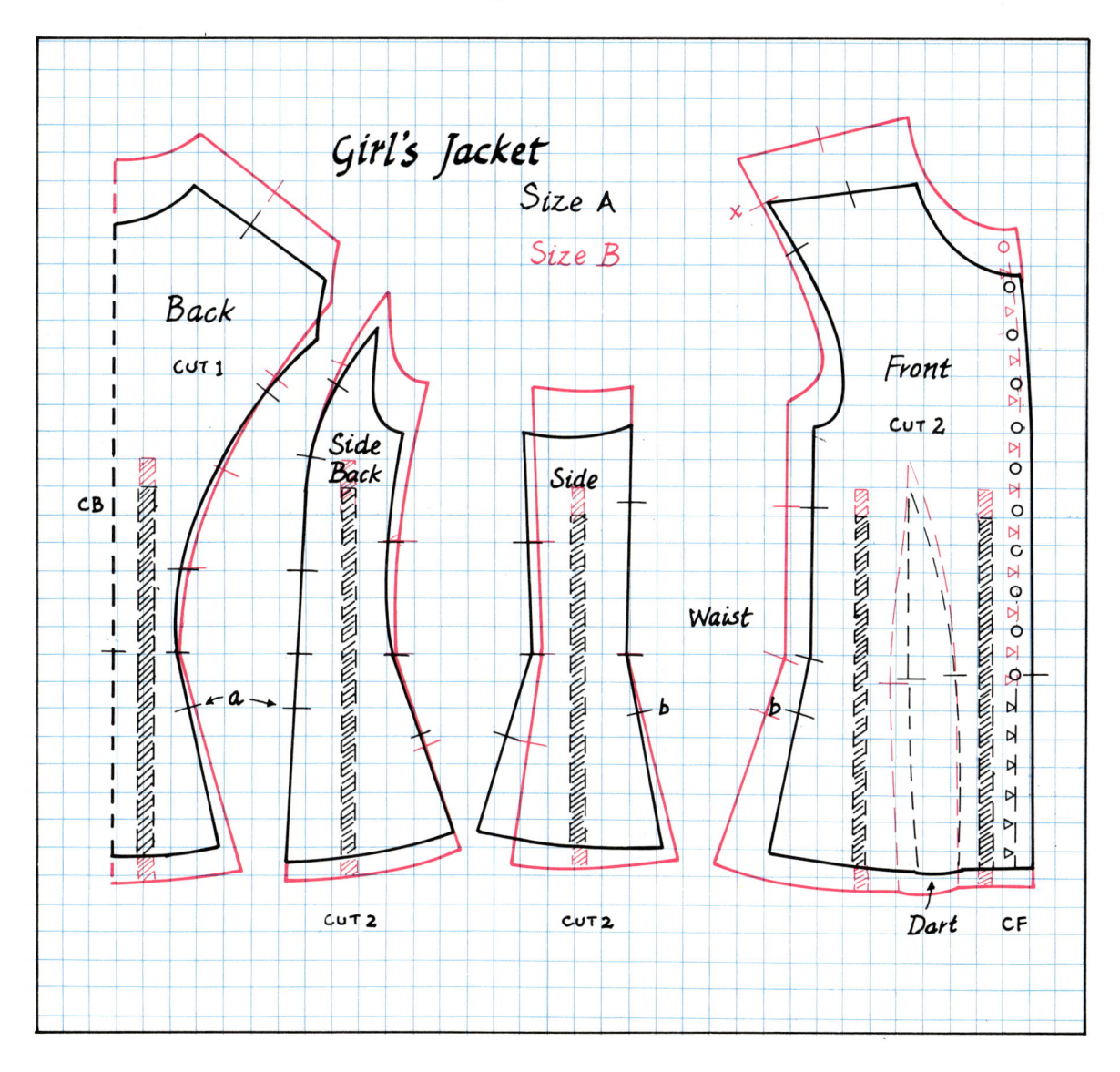

Girl's jacket

inside centre front line, following shape of front edge. Cut out this shape and use as a pattern to cut out facings in main fabric.

4 Sew Rigilene along bone lines on wrong side of lining material, stopping 1cm short of hem line.

5 Wrong sides together, tack main fabric to lining material just outside seam lines, and use as one fabric.

6 Stitch darts in both fronts and press.

7 Right sides together, sew facings to front edges along seam line.

8 Turn to inside along seam line (*not* centre front line) and press. Edge stitch.

9 Right sides together and matching balance marks, join side fronts to front.

10 Right sides together and matching balance marks, join side backs to backs, leaving open from balance mark 'a' to bottom hem. The seam should be curved.

11 Right sides together and matching balance marks, join backs.

12 Right sides together and matching balance marks, join side fronts to side backs, leaving open from balance mark 'b' to hem.

13 Follow stages 10–13 of the instructions for the Evening Bodice.

14 Bias bind neck edge to neaten. Make and attach collar separately, according to the Large collar instructions on page 30.

15 Decorate by binding round edge of hem, including openings in sides, and up both fronts.

16 Sew in sleeves according to the plain sleeve instructions on page 18.

17 Make buttonholes down centre front line on *right* front, and sew buttons down left front to match, or make imitation buttonholes around buttons. The jacket can then be fastened with Velcro, press fasteners, or hooks and bars.

18 A blouse with a Peter Pan collar (see page 31) could be worn under the jacket, with the collar showing, instead of making a collar on the jacket.

Boy's green jacket and urchin's coat tails, 1850
Boy wears cropped jacket with collar; trousers.
'Urchin' wears basic 'uniform' jacket with tails; one-piece sleeves; trousers.

Cropped jacket, and tails, 1850   23

BOY'S CROPPED JACKET

A green cropped jacket ('cropped' means short) may be seen in the picture on page 23. This type of jacket was often worn by younger boys. It fastened at the neck with a button or hook and loop, or hook and bar. Jackets were usually dark, in a fabric such as cotton, wool, linen, or velvet.

The pattern given below is for a jacket to the waist, but it can easily be lengthened to reach the hips, like the one illustrated in the picture.

1. Make calico pattern as instructed in Fitting Guide, adding 5cm for turnings on front, side and back seams, and 2cm on all other seams.
2. Using corrected calico pattern, cut out main fabric.
3. Use a tracing wheel and dressmakers' tracing paper to trace pattern outlines and markings on to wrong side of fabric.
4. Right sides together and matching balance marks, join side seams.
5. Right sides together and matching balance marks, join centre back seam.
6. Right sides together and matching balance marks, join shoulder seams.
7. Turn in 5cm on each front edge, and press.
8. Edge stitch, neaten raw edges, and stitch down.
9. Bias bind neck edge, or neaten.
10. Make and attach collar if required, according to the instructions on page 31.
11. Turn up bottom hem and stitch, or neaten with bias binding.
12. Sew on button and loop or hook and eye to fasten at neck.

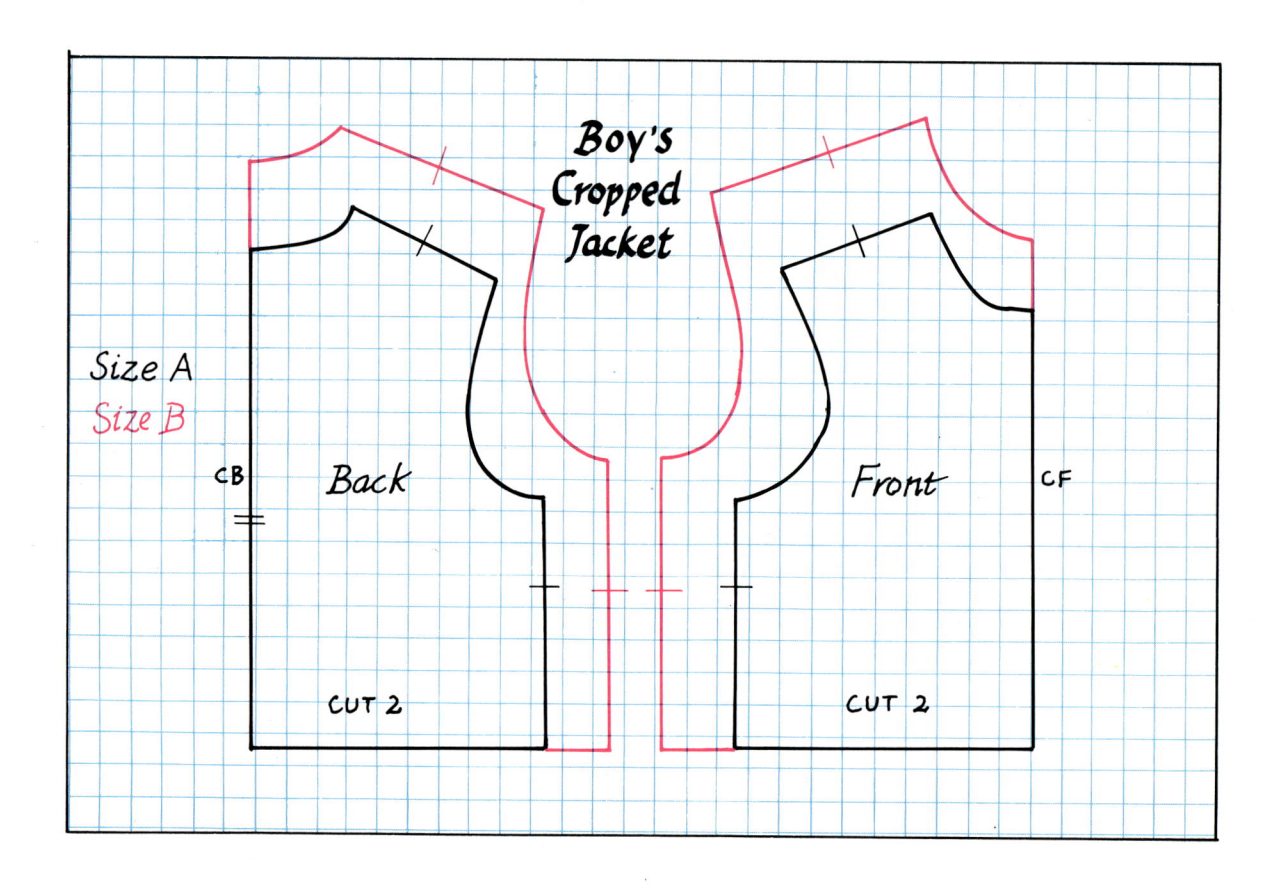

Army officers' uniform 25

Army officer's uniform, about 1860
Uniform jacket with one-piece sleeves with cuffs, collar, and uniform 'skirt'. Trousers.

MAN'S COAT OR UNIFORM JACKET

The pattern which follows is equally suitable for the green 1837 coat illustrated on page 29 and the 1860 uniform jacket on page 25. The skirt patterns, sleeves, and cuffs, are altered as necessary. For the 1837 coat, a firm but soft fabric such as wool would be suitable. The uniform jacket will look best if it is lined in the same way as the ladies' bodices, using a firm lining such as drill. A very firm fabric looks smartest for this jacket, but you might be able to use felt if it is well lined. The urchin's coat shown in the illustration on page 23 is also based on this pattern.

1. Make calico pattern as instructed in Fitting Guide, adding 5cm for turnings on centre back and straight side seams on front and side pattern pieces, and 2cm for turnings on all other seams and edges.

2. Using corrected calico pattern, cut out lining fabric.

3. Use a tracing wheel and dressmakers' tracing paper to trace pattern outlines and markings on to right side of lining fabric.

4. Use this as a pattern to cut out main fabric. Make sure the pieces are the right way round, and that you have right and left sides, right and left sleeves, etc.

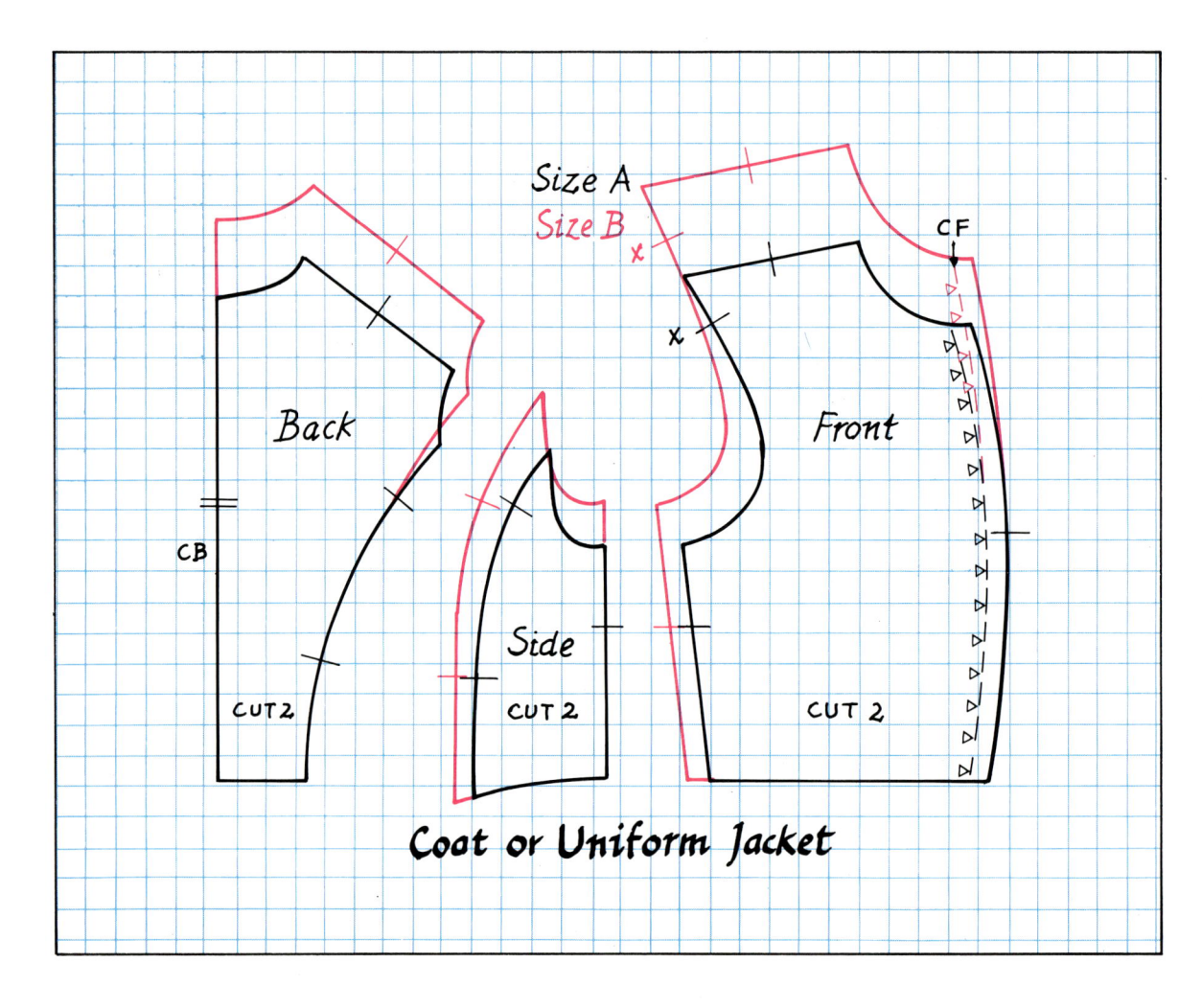

Coat or Uniform Jacket

5. To cut pattern for front facings, use corrected calico pattern for front. Draw a line 5cm inside centre front line, following shape of front edge. Cut out this shape and use as a pattern to cut out facings in main fabric.
6. Wrong sides together, tack main fabric to lining material just outside seam lines, and use as one fabric.
7. Right sides together, sew facings to front edges along seam line.
8. Turn to inside along seam line (*not* centre front line) and press. Edge stitch.
9. Right sides together and matching balance marks, join sides to backs. The seam should be curved.
10. Right sides together and matching balance marks, join sides to fronts.
11. Right sides together and matching balance marks, join backs.
12. Right sides together and matching balance marks, join shoulder seams.
13. Clip curves and zig-zag or oversew raw edges to neaten.
14. Press all seams open.
15. Make buttonholes down centre front line on *left* front, and sew buttons down right front to match, or make imitation buttonholes around buttons. The jacket can then be fastened with Velcro, press fasteners, or hooks and bars.
16. Add skirt (see page 27).
17. Add collar (see pages 30 and 31).
18. Add one-piece sleeves (see page 18).
19. Decorate a uniform jacket with gold or silver braid.

SKIRTS FOR MEN'S COATS AND UNIFORM JACKETS

Coat skirt

This is shown in the picture of the green 1837 coat on page 29.

1. Measure from centre front of coat waist to centre back.
2. Multiply by 2 or 3 depending on thickness of material and fullness required.
3. Measure required length.
4. Cut two pieces of fabric to these measurements, adding 2cm for turnings all round.
5. Repeat stage 4 with lining fabric.
6. Right sides together, stitch one piece of fabric and one piece of lining together round three sides, leaving top open.
7. Clip corners, turn to right side, and press.
8. Pleat or gather each skirt to fit half of coat waist.
9. Stitch skirts to waist, press allowances up, and cover raw edges with tape or bias binding to neaten.

Uniform jacket skirt

This skirt is illustrated on page 25. It should be made of the same fabric as the body of the coat, and looks best if lined.

1. Make calico pattern as instructed in Fitting Guide, adding 2cm for turnings all round. Then use this pattern to cut out fabric and lining.
2. Right sides together, and matching balance marks, join side seams of fabric skirts. Do not join back seam.
3. Repeat stage 2 with lining.
4. Right sides together, join fabric and lining together round three sides, leaving waist edge open.
5. Clip corners, turn to right side, and press.
6. Right sides together, join waist edge of skirt fabric only (not lining) to waist of jacket.
7. Clip curves if necessary, press up turnings, and stitch lining over raw edge to neaten.

28　Coat and jacket skirts

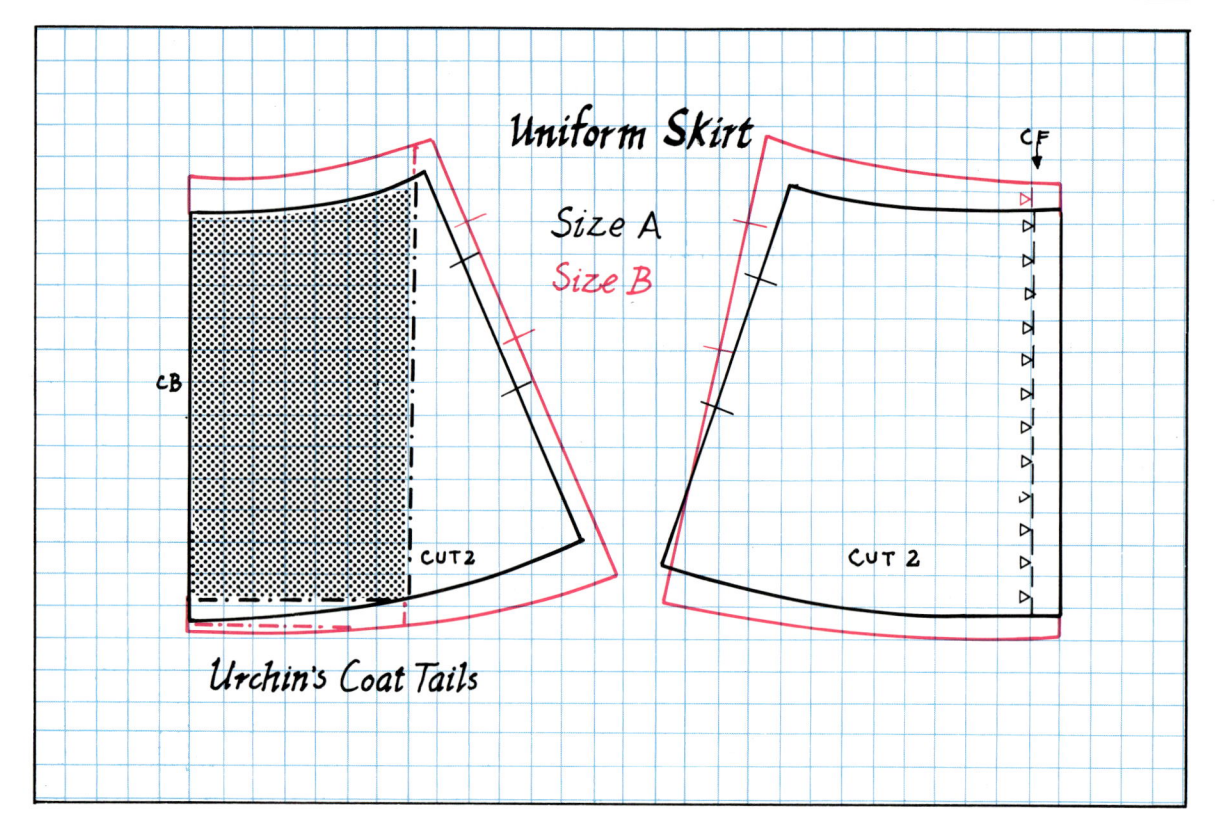

Uniform Skirt

Size A
Size B

CB
CUT 2
CF
CUT 2

Urchin's Coat Tails

Coat tails

Coat tails are illustrated in the picture of the poorly dressed urchin wearing a top hat shown on page 23. These tails are made in the same way as the uniform jacket skirt, using the narrow version of the pattern for the back panels.

1　Follow stage 1 of instructions for uniform jacket skirt, using pattern for back panels only.

2　Follow stages 4–7 of instructions for uniform jacket skirt.

3　Neaten front waist edge of coat with bias binding.

Green coat 29

Young man's green coat, about 1837
Coat made of uniform jacket, with one-piece sleeves with cuffs, large collar, and 'skirt'. Trousers.

COLLARS

Large collar

This collar is for the young man's coat illustrated on page 29.

1. Make calico pattern as instructed in Fitting Guide, adding 2cm turnings all round.
2. Using corrected calico pattern, cut out one collar in fabric and one collar in lining material.
3. Stiffen collar with iron-on Vilene if required.
4. Right sides together, stitch fabric and lining material together round outside edge of collar from 'b' to 'b'.
5. Clip into curves, turn to right side, and press.
6. Bias bind turning at neck edge of collar from 'b' to 'b'.
7. Stitch bound edge of collar inside neck edge of coat, matching centre fronts, and matching 'a' to shoulder seam of coat.

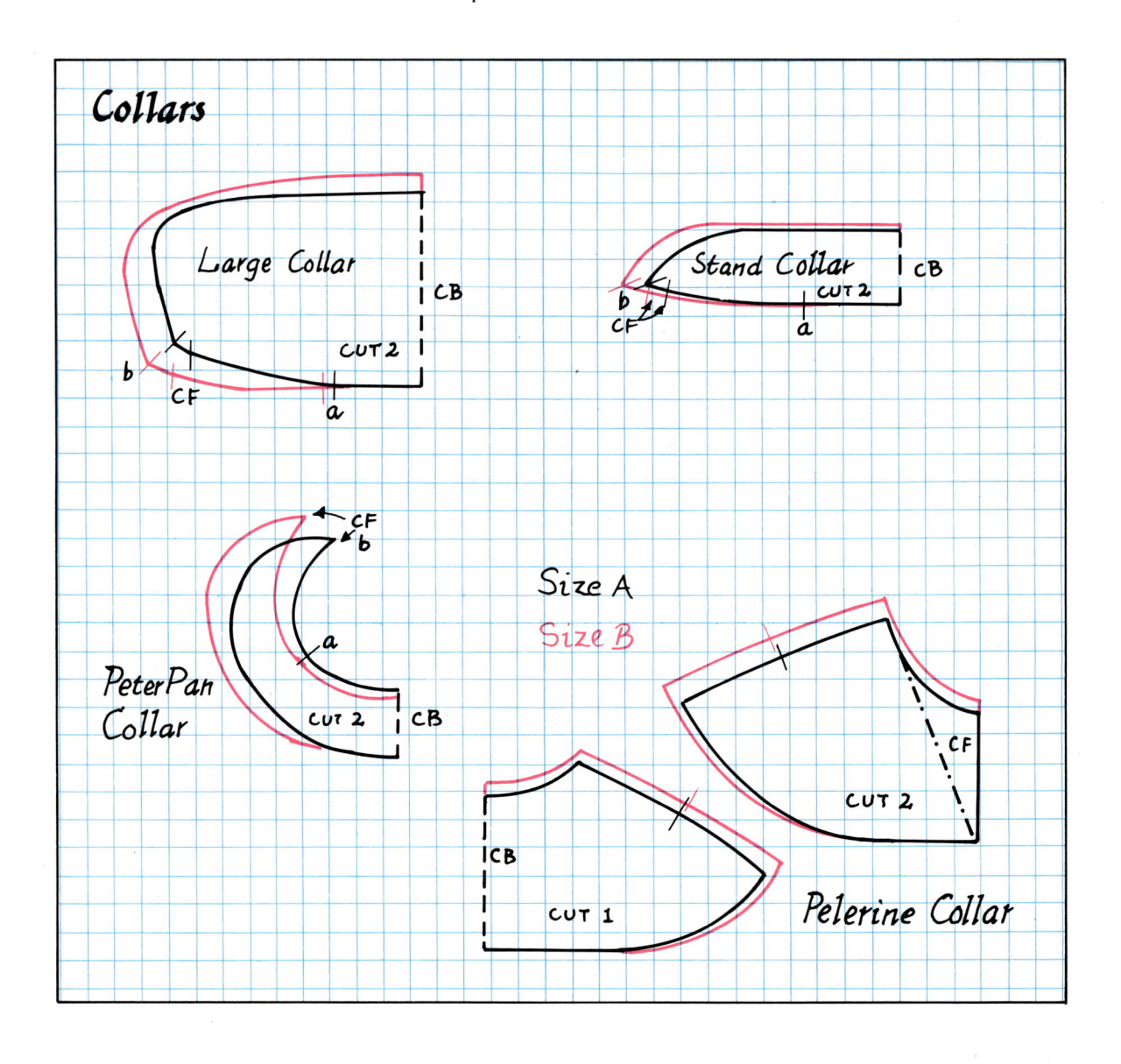

Collars

Stand collar

This collar should be used for the uniform jacket on page 25. It should be quite stiff, so more than one layer of iron-on Vilene may be needed.

1. Follow stages 1–5 of instructions for large collar.
2. Right sides together, and matching 'a' to shoulder seam, stitch collar fabric only (not lining) to neck edge of jacket.
3. Clip into curves and press up turnings into collar.
4. Stitch down lining to cover raw edges.
5. Trim edge of collar with braid to match braid on jacket.

Peter Pan collar

This collar is the one to use for the girl's jacket on page 19 and the boy's cropped jacket on page 23. It can be made in the same fabric as the coat or jacket, or in a washable cotton-type fabric, so that it can then be taken off and washed when required. If being used for a lady's dress or jacket, it can be trimmed with lace.

Follow instructions as for the Large collar on page 30, making sure that the points are pushed out neatly.

Pelerine collar

A pelerine collar was a large collar rather like a shawl, which often had long front ends. The collar shown on the tan day dress (page 7) is a very simple version.

This collar is made in two layers of a fine fabric such as voile or organza, and can be trimmed with lace. If the fabric used is not very fine, it may be better to use one layer only. Two variations of the front edge are given in the pattern.

1. Make calico pattern as instructed in Fitting Guide, adding 2cm turnings all round.
2. Using corrected calico pattern, cut out collar twice in fine fabric, to give the two layers.
3. Sew one layer at a time. Right sides together and matching balance marks, join shoulder seams of one layer.
4. Repeat with second layer.
5. Right sides together, join the two layers together down centre front edge, round curved edge and up other centre front edge.
6. Bag out, clipping into curves, and press.
7. Bias bind turning at neck edge, and stitch binding to inside neck of bodice.
8. Trim collar with lace if required, and fasten with a bow.

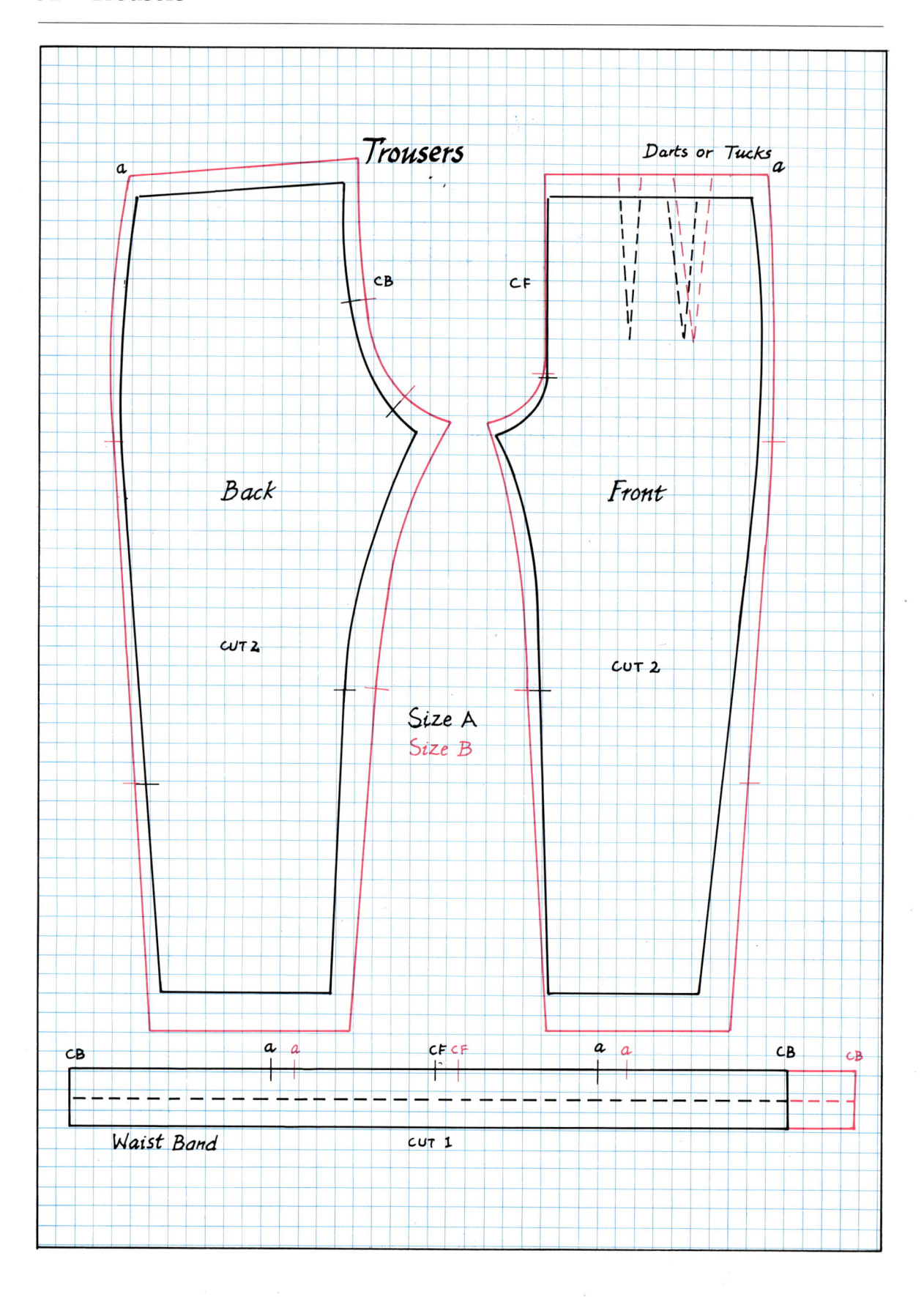

Trousers

TROUSERS

These trousers, often made of a light coloured material such as cotton or linen, are suitable for older boys and young men. They are seen in the pictures on pages 25 and 29, and both figures on page 23.

1. Make calico pattern as instructed in Fitting Guide, adding 5cm for turnings on front and back seams and bottom hem, and 2cm on all other seams. These trousers are a close fit so it is very important, when fitting the calico pattern, to make sure that the stretched waistband is big enough to pull up over the hips.
2. Using corrected calico pattern, cut out main fabric.
3. Use a tracing wheel and dressmakers' tracing paper to trace pattern outlines and markings on to wrong side of fabric.
4. Stitch up darts, or tack tucks.
5. Right sides together and matching balance marks, join centre back seam.
6. Right sides together and matching balance marks, join centre front seam.
7. Right sides together and matching balance marks, join side seams.
8. Right sides together and matching balance marks, join inside leg seams, starting at one ankle, stitching up to crutch, then down to other ankle.
9. Join ends of waistband in to a circle.
10. Right sides together and matching balance marks, stitch waistband to waist of trousers.
11. Turn to inside along fold and edge stitch.
12. Turn allowance under and stitch down, leaving an opening at each side for elastic.
13. Stitch elastic firmly inside waistband at one side seam, thread through back waistband, and stitch firmly at other side seam.
14. Stitch up openings.
15. Turn legs up to required length and stitch hem. (The hem should just reach the ankle for younger boys.)
16. If these trousers are to be used as part of a uniform, a line of coloured wool braid, or gold or silver braid, can be sewn down the outside seams.

CRINOLINE

A crinoline was a metal frame worn under a lady's skirt to hold it out to a very full shape. The use of the metal crinoline began in 1856 and lasted, with variations, for 10–15 years. However, all the dresses in this book may be worn over a crinoline if required, as the frame helps to keep the skirt material away from the legs. The crinoline may be made

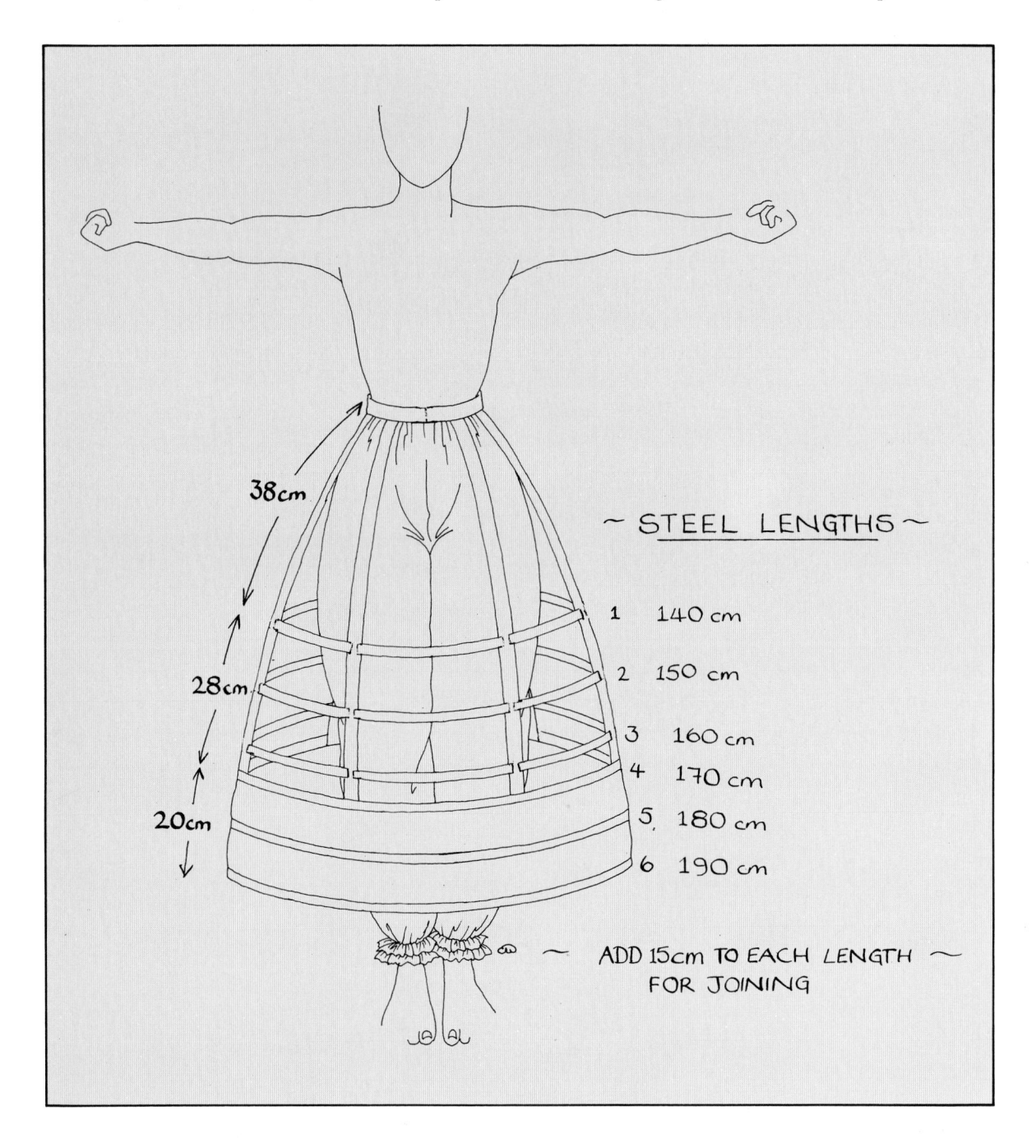

~ STEEL LENGTHS ~

1 140 cm
2 150 cm
3 160 cm
4 170 cm
5 180 cm
6 190 cm

~ ADD 15cm TO EACH LENGTH ~
FOR JOINING

38cm
28cm
20cm

Crinoline

smaller or larger by altering the size of each metal 'hoop' in proportion.

The crinoline shown in the diagram is a fairly simple shape, and gives a full-skirted look. Unless the skirt is made of a very thick fabric, a petticoat should be worn over the crinoline to prevent the steel hoops showing through.

Cutting and fastening the crinoline steel should only be done under supervision, because the steel is extremely sharp. It may be better to use cane if it is available.

Basic crinoline

1. Cut a strip of calico 2m long and 44cm wide, joining pieces to make this size if necessary.
2. Join short ends to make a circle, press seam, and zig-zag raw edges flat to calico.
3. Wrong sides together, fold calico strip in half length-ways and edge stitch along fold.
4. Sew a row of stitches 2cm above this line to make a channel for steel. Do not stitch completely round, but leave a gap to thread steel.
5. Repeat rows of stitching halfway up strip to make next channel.
6. Cut seven lengths of curtain heading tape to approximately 70cm. (Make sure steel will thread through tape loops).
7. Pull out drawstrings.
8. Fold top edges of calico strip to inside for 3cm and press.
9. Pin one end of each tape between edges of calico strip at equal intervals, about 25cm apart. It is important to make sure that spaces in tape are level all round, otherwise steel cannot be fitted properly.
10. Stitch edges of calico strip together by turning allowance to inside of strip and edge stitching, leaving a gap of at least 15cm to thread steel.
11. Make a row of stitches 2cm below edge stitching.
12. Cut petersham for waistband. Pin loose ends of tape to waistband at equal intervals all round. Make sure each tape *has the same number of spaces from waist to strip*, otherwise crinoline will not hang correctly.
13. Complete waistband as described in Glossary.
14. Make openings in seam of calico strip to thread the steels or canes.
15. If using cane, soften in water before using. The ends should be cut slanting using a sharp knife. Allow about 10cm for overlap. Thread through channels in calico strip, and through spaces in tapes. Overlap ends and bind together with PVC or insulating tape.
16. If using crinoline steel, cut with steel cutters, allowing 15cm for overlap. Cover ends with zinc oxide tape, then cover tape with Sellotape or PVC tape. Thread through channels in calico strip and through spaces in tapes, overlap, and bind ends together with zinc oxide tape.
17. Stitch up gaps in calico strip. Approximate lengths of steels/canes are shown on the diagram. Overlap of 15cm must be added.

The length may be adjusted by shortening the tapes evenly all round, but care must be taken not to change the proportions, so the steels may have to be shortened too. The crinoline should be about 10–15cm off the floor.

Crinoline pad

A pad may be worn under the back of the crinoline to make the back stick out further. It may also be worn on its own under a petticoat if a crinoline is not worn. It is made of calico.

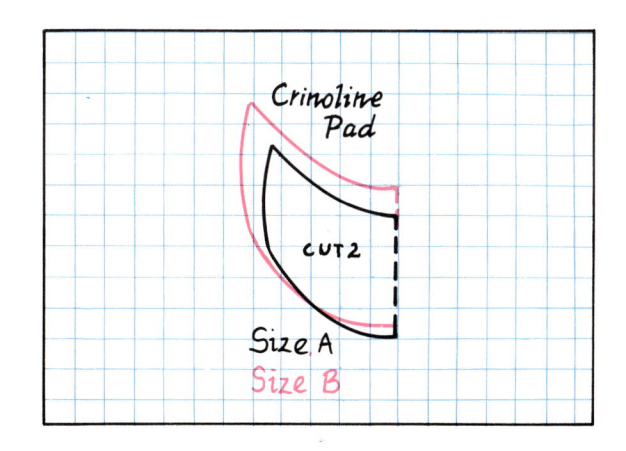

Crinoline

1. Cut out pad, allowing 2cm turnings all round.
2. Stitch round, leaving a gap on outside edge. Clip into curves, and turn to right side.
3. Stuff firmly with kapok or wadding, and stitch up gap.
4. Attach by points to inside back waist of crinoline.

Crinoline frills

Frills added to a crinoline skirt give it a richer, flouncey look. You can see frills on the green dress on page 38 and the lilac dress on page 11.

1. Multiply required width by 2 for a loose frill, or by 3 for a bunchier frill.
2. Cut a strip of calico, marquisette, or stiff net to this measurement by the required depth, adding 2cm for turnings all round.
3. Turn a narrow hem all round and stitch.
4. Gather top of frill over piping cord, draw up to required width, and stitch down, hiding piping cord between frill and fabric.

A crinoline for the white evening dress on page 37 can be easily adapted from the basic crinoline by adding a set of frills of calico or marquisette, either to the crinoline itself or to the petticoat. The frills should be detachable (use Velcro or poppers) so that the crinoline or petticoat can be used for other dresses.

1. Cut a piece of calico 24cm by 24cm, and turn and stitch a narrow hem all round.
2. Make three frills as described above, 20cm by 10cm finished when gathered.
3. Stitch bottom frill along bottom of calico, middle frill about 4.5cm up from bottom, and top frill about 7.5cm down from top edge.
4. Pleat top edge to 15cm and stitch to long tape to tie round waist.
5. Stitch poppers or Velcro to bottom inside edge of calico piece.
6. Stitch poppers or Velcro to crinoline tapes or centre back of petticoat to match.

Evening dress, 1865 37

Woman's evening dress in white with red trim, about 1865
Evening dress bodice with evening sleeves (shaped version) and bertha. Two skirts with single frill over crinoline and petticoat.

38 Evening dress, about 1842

Young woman's green evening dress, about 1842
Evening bodice with evening sleeves and lace bertha. Skirt with two frills over petticoat and crinoline.

PETTICOAT

A petticoat is an underskirt which holds out a skirt to make it look fuller. It should be made of cheap material like calico or sheeting. A pattern is not necessary. If worn over a crinoline it should be about 15cm bigger than the crinoline, and 5–7cm longer when finished, and it should have a frill. Whether or not a crinoline is worn, a petticoat is always advisable.

1. Using above measurements as a guide, cut calico to size, adding 7.5cm for hem and 7.5cm to shape top.
2. Join to make a tube, leaving an opening in one seam for centre back fastening.
3. Press seams and neaten raw edges.
4. Neaten back opening with placket, and turn up hem.
5. Stitch on frill, which should be 2–3 times the width of the petticoat hem, and about 20cm deep. The hem of the frill should hang 1cm below the hem of the petticoat.
6. Gather waist edge of calico over piping cord about 7.5cm from top. Keep centre front waist flat for about 10cm, spreading gathers evenly along remaining waistband.
7. Try on, over crinoline or pad if using, and adjust length from top. Hem should be level with floor.
8. Finish waist.

SKIRTS

Most of the skirts illustrated are made in exactly the same way as the petticoats. The length of the skirt depends on the period and on the age and status of the character wearing the costume. This can be checked by looking at original drawings, paintings, fashion plates, and other pictures of the period required. The skirt should be made up on a waistband (see Glossary). The bodice should then be stitched through to the waistband, unless the waist of the bodice is curved, in which case a sash or belt can cover the join.

Plain skirt

The plain skirt is suitable for the dresses of 1835 (page 4) and 1837 (page 7), and the skirt of the 1845 suit (page 19). Use the same skirt for the pink-checked day dress (page 41), but cut it shorter, keeping the hem level with the ground. The skirt is made in exactly the same way as the petticoat. It should be worn over a petticoat trimmed with a 20cm deep frill. The hem should be about 2.25m round for the smaller size, and 2.7m for the larger size.

Skirt with two frills

This type of skirt is shown on the green evening dress of 1842 (page 38). The basic skirt is made in exactly the same way as the petticoat. The hem should be 3.15m round for the smaller size, and 3.6m for the larger size. Each frill is 1.5 times the width of the hem, and the finished depth is about 20cm. The bottom frill should be sewn on first, and the top frill should be sewn on so that its hem just covers the top of the bottom frill. The top of the frill should be turned to the inside before stitching, to hide piping cord.

Double skirt

This skirt is for the 1865 white evening dress on page 37. It is actually two skirts, both made in exactly the same way as the basic petticoat. The hem should be about 3.15m round for the smaller size, and about 3.6m for the larger size. The skirt should be worn over a crinoline and petticoat which may both need frills down the back to give the shape shown in the illustration.

1. Make up two skirts as for petticoat.
2. Make up frills, each twice hem width and 15cm finished depth. Sew on as for frilled skirt.
3. Mark waistband in quarters, centre front, sides and back.
4. Mark both skirt waists in quarters
5. Pin waist of underskirt to waistband, spreading 30cm of skirt fabric from the front half of waistband to back half to make back skirt fuller. Keep centre front flat for about 10cm, as for petticoat.
6. Try on skirt and check hem length before starting top skirt.
7. Pin a length of tape to waist band to hang down skirt at side quarters, and repeat stage 5 with top skirt.
8. Complete waistband.
9. Put skirt on over crinoline and petticoat and pull top skirt up as shown in the illustration on page 37.
10. Stitch through to tapes, neaten tape ends, and cover stitches with bow.
11. Attach to bodice as above.

Shaped skirt with three frills

The shaped skirt is seen on the lilac day dress of 1858 (page 11). It is best worn over a crinoline and petticoat, which should have a 20cm deep frill at the bottom. The hem should be about 2.25m round for the smaller size, and about 2.7m for the larger size. The petticoat will need one or two rows of marquisette or stiff net frills at the hem.

1. The basic skirt is made in exactly the same way as the petticoat, but the fullness at the waist can be reduced by four long darts.
2. The bottom frill should be 2.5 times hem width, the middle frill 2 times hem width, and the top frill 1.5 times hem width.
3. To work out depth of frills for day dress, measure skirt from 10cm below waist to hem, and divide by 3.
4. Add 7.5cm for overlap, 2.5cm for top hem, and 2.5cm for bottom hem unless using a border print.
5. Turn hems at top and bottom of each frill and gather over piping cord to fit skirt.
6. Sew bottom frill on first, then middle frill, allowing an overlap of 7.5cm. Sew top frill on last, turning top to inside to hide piping cord. Top of top frill should be about 10cm down from waist.
7. Make up skirt on to waistband, keeping hem level with floor.

It is important to check all skirt lengths by trying the skirt on with the crinoline or petticoat, otherwise you may find the skirt is too short.

Day dress, about 1850   41

Girl's pink-checked day dress, about 1850
Closed bodice with pagoda sleeves and pagoda sleeve puffs. Plain skirt worn over petticoat and pantaloons.

42 Pantaloons

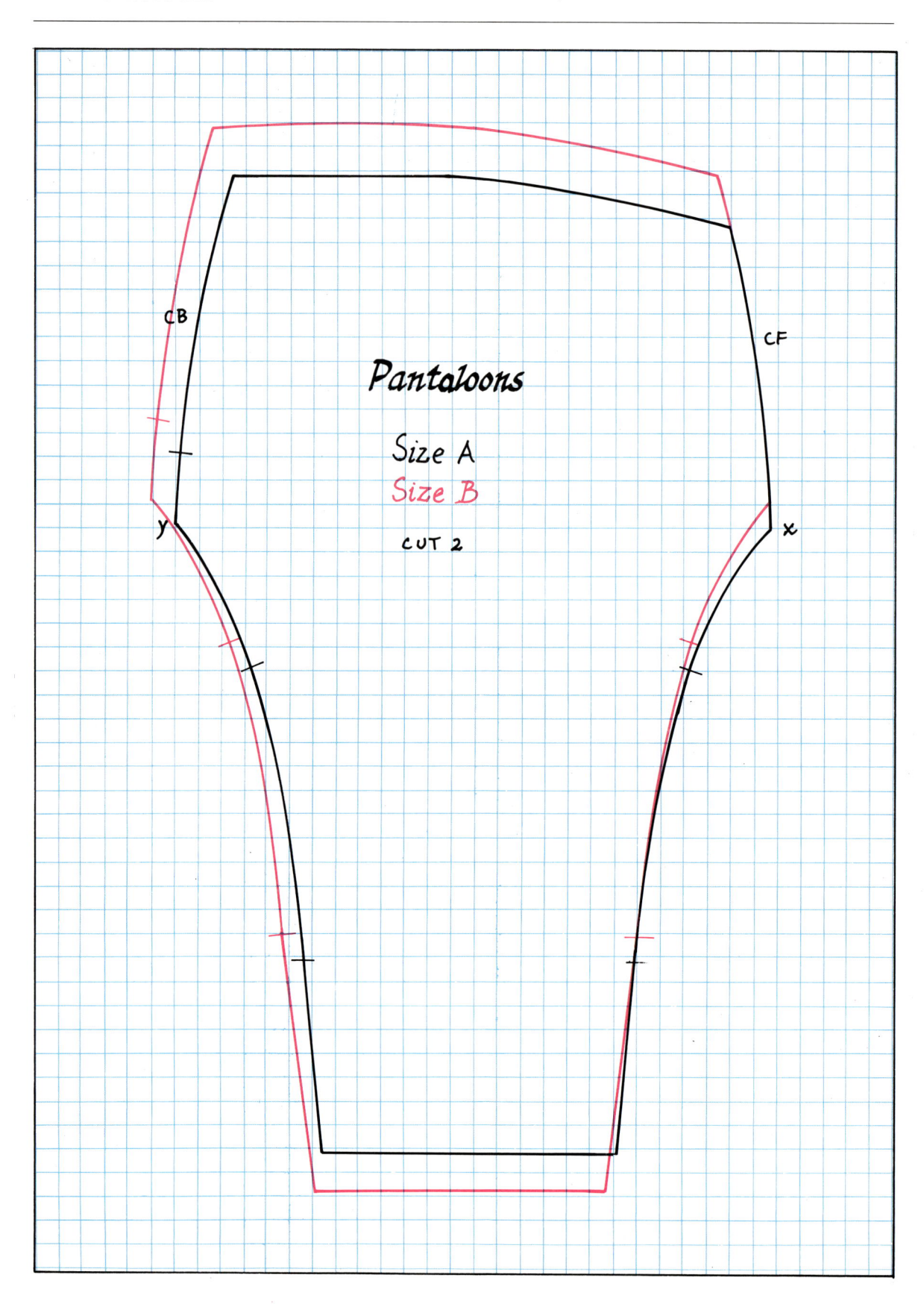

PANTALOONS

Pantaloons were a type of trousers worn under the skirts of women, girls, and small boys. Costumes for small children usually have skirts to just below the knee with pantaloons showing, as you can see in the picture of the girl on page 41. The edge of the pantaloons sometimes showed beneath the ankle-length skirts of older girls and women, as in the illustration of the tan day dress on page 7.

Pantaloons were made of linen or cotton, or possibly silk, perhaps trimmed with lace or broderie anglaise. Boys wore fairly plain ones. The fabrics for pantaloons are quite cheap, so it should not be necessary to make a calico pattern first.

This pattern is for ankle-length pantaloons but can be adjusted for a shorter length.

1. Make paper pattern as instructed in Fitting Guide, adding 2cm for turnings on all seams, and 5cm on waist edge and on hem. Then use this to cut out the fabric.
2. Use a tracing wheel and dressmakers' tracing paper to trace pattern outlines and markings to wrong side of fabric.
3. Right sides together and matching balance marks, join centre front seams from waist to 'x'.
4. Right sides together and matching balance marks, join centre back seams from balance marks to 'y'.
5. Press seam allowance to inside, neaten raw edges, and edge stitch.
6. Right sides together and matching balance marks, join inside leg seams, starting at one ankle, stitching up to crutch, then down to other ankle.
7. Press seams and neaten raw edges.
8. Turn waist seam allowance to inside, turn in raw edge and stitch down, leaving centre back ends open to thread draw string.
9. Thread strong tape or ribbon through waistband, and stitch to waistband at centre front seam to stop it pulling out.
10. Turn up bottom hem edge and stitch.
11. Thread elastic through bottom hem if gathered effect is required.
12. Decorate with lace or broderie anglaise.

GLOSSARY

BAG OUT A way of lining sleeves and collars neatly. Right sides together, sew the lining and main fabric together along three sides. Trim allowances to 6mm, clip corners, turn inside out, and press.

BALANCE MARKS Markings on the pattern which are matched so that the separate pieces fit together properly.

BERTHA See page 15.

BIAS BINDING A type of binding used for turning up and neatening hems and edges. Open one fold of the binding and pin to right side of hem. Stitch along crease line (diagram a). Then fold to enclose raw edge and stitch (b), or turn up completely to inside and stitch (c).

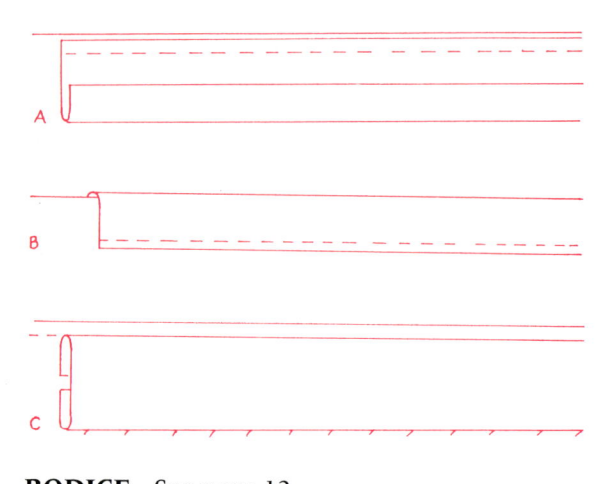

BODICE See page 12.

BRODERIE ANGLAISE A type of embroidered cotton suitable for trimming underwear.

CALICO A firm cotton fabric suitable for petticoats, or for lining bodices which need boning in which case it should be shrunk by washing before use. As it is a cheap fabric it is also used to make up the pattern on which the final garment is based.

CANE Pliable rods, available from craft shops, used to make crinoline hoops (see page 34.)

CLIPPING INTO CURVES/CORNERS Cut seam allowance almost to stitch line, about 2cm apart, to ease material round curve or corner.

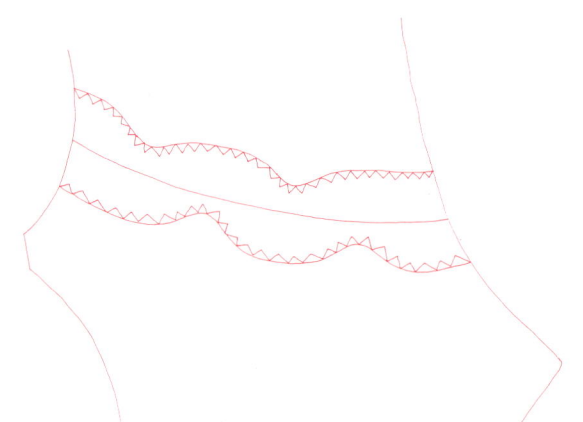

CRINOLINE See page 34.

CRINOLINE STEEL Pliable steel strips used to make crinoline hoops (see page 34).

DARTS A stitched fold in the material, used for shaping a garment. Sew from wide end to point. If the material is thick, the dart may be cut along the fold to 1cm from the point, and pressed open.

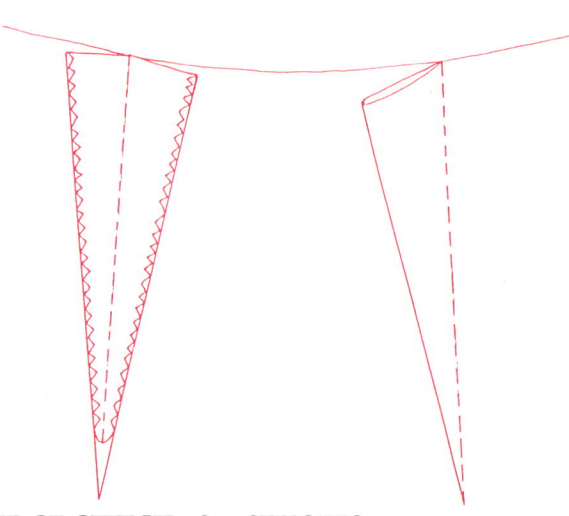

EDGE STITCH See STITCHES

FACING A method of making neat edges on the front of a garment by lining them with a piece of fabric.

GATHERING Make a row of stitches each side of the marked line. Pull up to fit

Glossary

measurements and stitch down between rows. If outer row of gathering stitches shows on right side, it can be removed.

HOOKS AND BARS, EYES, OR LOOPS Used for fastening. Set hooks about 2mm from the edge of the material and sew down firmly through the holes. Sew the hook end down firmly. If using loops, leave the loop protruding over the edge of the material by about 2mm. Stitch down firmly.

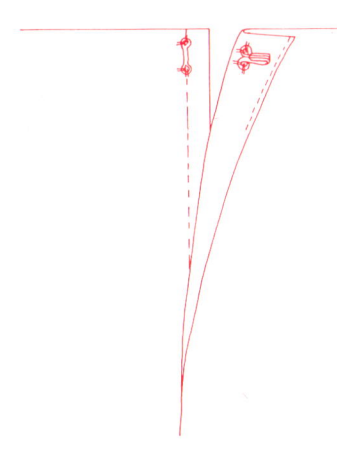

INDIA TAPE Firm cotton tape for ties or making channels for steels on crinoline.

MARQUISETTE A stiff, open-weave fabric suitable for stiffening sleeves, etc.

PATTERN See page 6.

PETERSHAM A firm tape used for waistbands.

PIPING CORD For gathering over a piping cord, use a wide zig-zag stitch on a sewing machine. Zig-zag over a piping cord or length of fine string. Pull up cord or string to fit. This is suitable for skirt waists or the heads of very full sleeves.

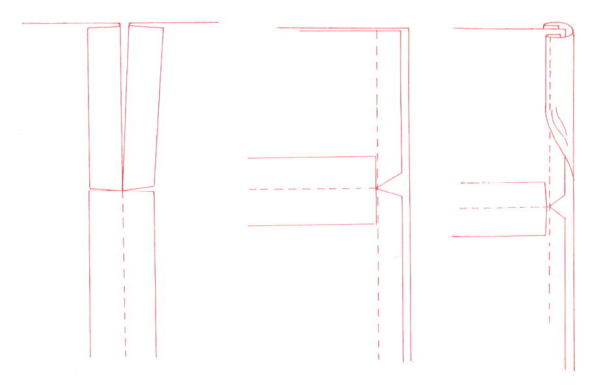

PLACKET A finished opening in a seam, usually a skirt. Cut strip of fabric twice length of opening and 6cm wide, plus 4cm all round for turnings. Clip seam allowance at bottom of opening. Right sides together, sew the strip to fabric, going backwards and forwards across seam to reinforce. Turn in raw edge, fold at wrong side to cover seam allowances, and stitch down. Press.

PLEATS Folds of definite, even width made by doubling cloth upon itself, and fastening in place.

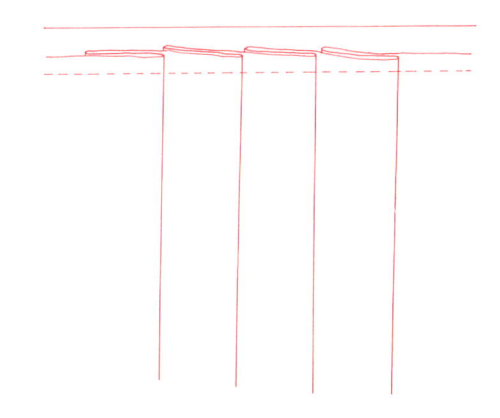

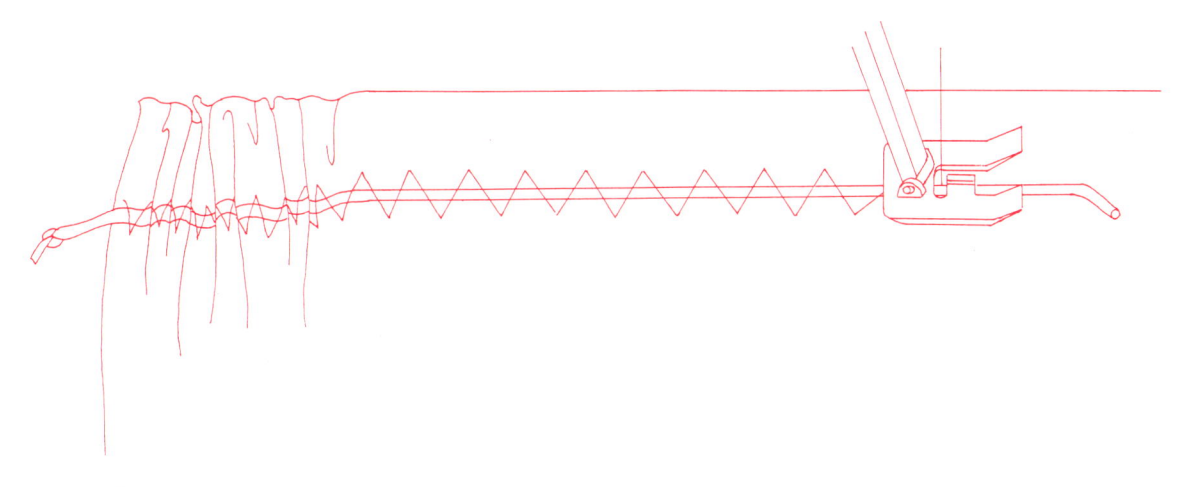

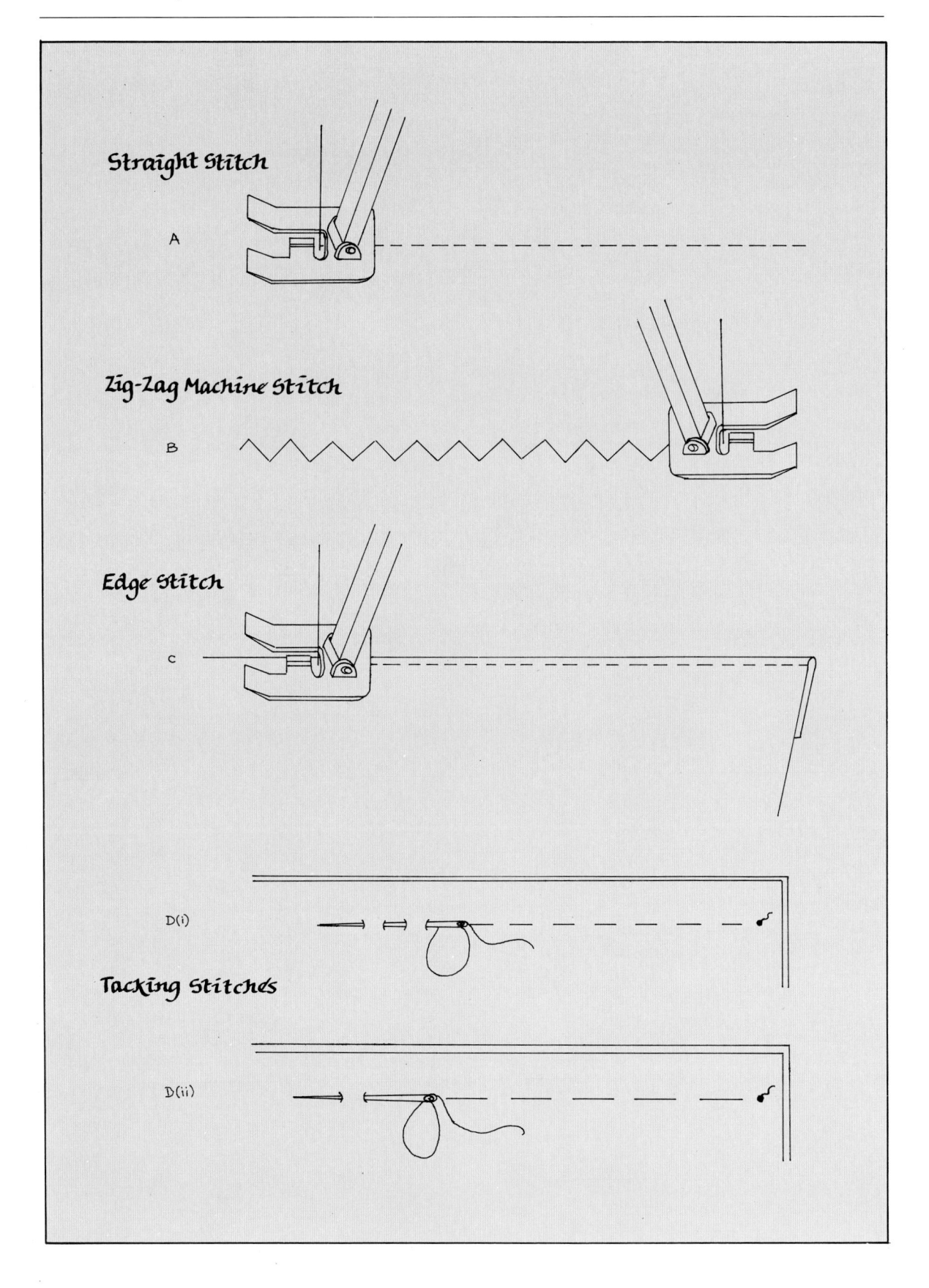

Glossary

Straight Stitch
A

Zig-Zag Machine Stitch
B

Edge Stitch
C

D(i)

Tacking Stitches

D(ii)

Glossary

POPPERS, PRESS FASTENERS A form of fastener in which one part is snapped into place inside the other.

RAW EDGE Unstitched edge.

RIGILENE Nylon boning, a modern substitute for whalebone or steel bones, but not so rigid. Cut to required length, and melt the ends in a candle flame to seal them and stop the ends from poking out. Sew to material along flat edge.

STITCHES *Straight stitch*: Used by hand or machine to join two pieces of material together. Usually for hems and seams (a).
Zig-Zag machine stitch: Used to neaten raw edges, or over piping cord for gathering (b).
Edge stitch: A row of stitches, usually machined 3mm from folded edge of material to strengthen (c).
Tacking stitch: Used to hold two pieces of material together to be used as one. Also used instead of pinning material together. Can be short stitches (d 1) or long stitches (d 2).
Topstitch: A row of stitches made on the right side of the material, usually close to the fold or to the seam, to hold and decorate the material.

STRAIGHT GRAIN The thread of the fabric which runs up and down, parallel to the selvedge. The straight grain runs up and down on most pattern pieces in this book, but each piece should be individually checked.

STRAIGHT STITCH See STITCHES

TACKING STITCH See STITCHES

TARLATAN A thin cotton fabric, slightly stiff, suitable for stiffening sleeves lightly.

TOPSTITCH See STITCHES

TRACING PAPER Dressmakers' coloured paper used to transfer information from the pattern to the material. It can be bought in packets with instructions and is used with a spiked tracing wheel.

VELCRO A fastener consisting of nylon loops meshed together. Useful for quick changes of clothes, but not really suitable for permanent fastenings. Sew along flat edges, and across both ends.

VILENE A type of stiffening in various strengths, available from dressmakers' shops. Can be 'sew-in' or 'iron-on'.

WAISTBAND The part of the garment encircling the waist. Usually best made on petersham. Cut to length plus at least 3cm for underlap, plus two 1.5cm turnings.

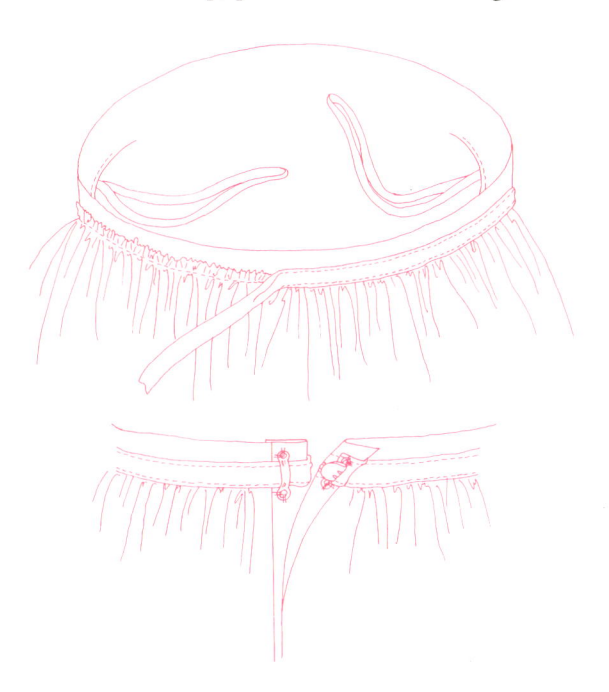

Before making up, sew on two 10cm loops at the sides for hanging up the garment. Sew the wrong side of the waist to the petersham (a). Cut off surplus material, turn in seam allowances of petersham and sew on twill or India tape to cover the raw edges. Finish with a trouser hook and bar. The petersham side is next to the body (b).

ZIG-ZAG MACHINE STITCH See STITCHES

INDEX

bagging out 44
balance marks 44
berthas 14, 15;
   illus 4, 37, 38
bias binding 44
bodices 10
   sleeves of 5
   see also closed bodice,
      evening bodice
broderie anglais 44

children's clothes 5
clipping into curves and
   corners 44
closed bodice 14–15;
   illus 7, 11, 41
coats 10;
   illus 29
coat skirt 27;
   illus 29
coat tails 28;
   illus 23
corsets 5
collars 30–31
   large 30
   pelerine 31;
      illus 7
   Peter Pan 31
   stand 31
   see also berthas

darts 44
drawers 5
dressmakers' tracing paper 9,
   47

evening bodice 12–13;
   illus 4, 37, 38
evening sleeve 18;
   illus 37, 38

fabrics 6, *see also under*
   individual garments
   amounts of 10

facing 44
fashion and style, reasons for
   change of 5
fitting guide 9–10

gathered sleeve 16;
   illus 7
gathering 44

hairstyles 6
hooks and bars, eyes, or loops
   44

India tape 45

jackets 10
   boys' 24;
      illus 23
   girls' 21–2;
      illus 19
   men's 26–7;
      illus 23, 25, 29
   skirts for 27;
      illus 25, 29
   tails for 28;
      illus 23
   uniform 26–7;
      illus 23, 25, 29

measuring 6–8

pagoda sleeve 16, 21;
   illus 11, 41
pantalettes and pantaloons 5, 43;
   illus 7, 41
patterns 6
   pattern-making 9–10
petersham tape 45
petticoats 5, 10, 39
piping cord 45
placket 45
pleats 45
poppers 45
puff sleeves 16;
   illus 4

Rigilene 45

skirts 39–40
   double 40;
   frills 39, 40;
      illus 11, 37, 38
   plain 39;
      illus 4, 7, 19, 41
sleeves 5, 10, 16–20
   cuffs 18;
      illus 19
   evening puff sleeve 16;
      illus 4
   evening sleeve 18;
      illus 37, 38
   gathered sleeve 16;
      illus 7
   pagoda sleeve 16, 21;
      illus 11, 41
   sleeve puff 16;
      illus 11, 41
   plain sleeve 18, 21;
      illus 19, 23, 25, 29
stitches 47
straight grain 47
style, reasons for change of 5

tailored clothes 5
trousers 32–3;
   illus 23, 25

uniform jacket 5, 26;
   illus 23
   skirt for 27

Velcro 47
Victorian period 5
   Early Victorian period
      defined 5
Vilene 47

waists 10, 47